CÁNTARO  LIBRARY

THE TEN COMMANDMENTS

CORNELIUS VAN TIL

Foreword by Steven R. Martins

cantaroinstitute.org | paideiapress.ca

The Ten Commandments
Co-published by Cántaro Publications, a publishing imprint of
Cántaro Institute, and Paideia Press, Jordan Station, ON.

The Ten Commandments © Cornelius Van Til, 1933.
This rare, never before published syllabus provides an exposition
of the ethics of the decalogue before John Murray began
teaching this course at WTS.

ISBN: 978-1-990771-37-8

Printed in Canada

CONTENTS

FOREWORD

WE LIVE IN A WORLD characterized by lawlessness. Not in the sense that the world has no laws by which it is governed—whether that be the arithmetical, kinematic, biotic, physical, logical, etc.—but in the sense that the natural man lives in rebellion against the revealed law of God. And what suffering this lawlessness has brought upon the world, *unspeakable* suffering when one surveys the history of mankind since the fall of our first parents. As we bear witness of the on-going consequence of man's disobedience—what the Scriptures refer to as "sin"—we realize the significance and necessity of the law of God for man's right living. In fact, what we would discover is that, to live in disobedience to the law of God brings about havoc and chaos one way or the other, it creates a violent disturbance—first in our hearts, and then rippling through every relationship that stems from it. But to live in obedience to the law of God provides the necessary conditions for the bearing of good fruit, peaceful relations, and human flourishment. When God gave the law to man—first by placing it in his heart by creating man in *His* image, and later handed down on stone tablets to the Israelites, *His* chosen people, and later expanded and applied through the writings of the prophet Moses, and then exemplified to the world through Israel's practice of it—He did it with the benefit of man in mind. Chiefly for His glory, no doubt, but certainly for the benefit of man. If we desire, as God's people in Christ, to live rightly, to live lawfully, to live righteously, to live in such a way that brings glory to our Creator God, then we must know the law of God. No, even more than that, we must *delight* in it. It was the Psalmist who wrote:

> Blessed is the man
> who walks not in the counsel of the
> wicked,
> nor stands in the way of sinners,
> nor sits in the seat of scoffers;
> but his delight is in the law of the LORD,
> and on his law he meditates day and
> night (Ps. 1:1-2).

Of course, there is a common question that emerges when we talk about the law of God. Is the law of God, as it was given in the Old Testament, still valid today? If we were to divide the law, as it is so commonly done today by theologians, into three categories, that being the moral, the civil, and the ceremonial, are all of these laws still valid? I address this question in significant detail in the seventh chapter of my book, *Apologetics: Studies in Biblical Apologetics for a Christian Worldview*, but for the present occasion, a brief answer will suffice.

Is the Law of God Still Valid Today?

This is a question that the Church has grappled with throughout the centuries. There are those who interpret Scripture to say that Jesus invalidated the law to make way for grace (what many *antinomians* believe). While others interpret Scripture saying that Jesus introduced a new law to replace the old, which most Christians call the "law of Christ." These are not the only positions, but they are perhaps the most well-known.

To answer the question of the validity of biblical law, we must take into account the literary and historical contexts of relevant biblical texts, the meaning behind the texts as they were given to us in their original language, and also what other passages have to say on the matter.

What did Jesus teach?

When asking about the validity of biblical law—the law established in the Old Testament—we can turn to the words of Jesus in the Sermon on the Mount.

> "Do not think that I have come to abolish the Law or the Prophets; I have not come to abolish them but to fulfill them. For truly, I say to you, until heaven and earth pass away, not an iota, not a dot, will pass from the Law until all is accomplished. Therefore whoever relaxes one of the least of these commandments and teaches others to do the same will be called least in the kingdom of heaven, but whoever does them and teaches them will be called great in the kingdom of heaven. For I tell you, unless your righteousness exceeds that of the scribes and Pharisees, you will never enter the kingdom of heaven" (Matt. 5:17-20).

That Jesus said this implies that the Jewish audience perceived His teaching as a new set of norms that could potentially replace the law of the Old Testament. As commentator John Nolland explains, "In Jewish terms, any attempt to annul (Gk. καταλύειν) the Law might have been viewed only with horror."[1]

Jesus is explaining the purpose of His miraculous incarnation. He entered the created world not to abolish "the law or the prophets," as the Jews might have believed, but to fulfill them. But what does the Greek πληρῶσαι for "fulfill" mean? The theologian R.J. Rushdoony writes that "fulfill" (*plērōsai*) means "to put into force [the law and the prophets]," arguing that any other interpretation does "violence to the clear meaning" of the text.[2]

In the first century, the Christian faith was "perceived as a new religion seeking to overthrow the ancestral law of the Jews," and because of this, it was Matthew's primary concern to "place the law and the prophets in the closest possible connection." He wanted both the Law and the Prophets to be close to Jesus since he understood that the

---

1. John Nolland, NIGTC: *The Gospel of Matthew*, (Grand Rapids, MI.: Wm. B. Eerdmans Publishing Company, 2005), 217.

2. R. J. Rushdoony, "*Jesus and the Law – Research*", *Chalcedon: Equipping to Advance the Kingdom*, 2010, Accessed September 8, 2016, http://chalcedon.edu/research/articles/jesus-and-the-law/.

prophetic allowed the Law to be correctly apprehended, and both are fully fulfilled in Christ.[3]

In Matthew 5:18, Jesus demonstrates His authority as a Lawgiver and King, stating: "For truly, I say to you, until heaven and earth pass away, not an iota, not a dot, will pass from the Law until all is accomplished." In other words, even if the entire creation were to cease to exist, what God has spoken in the Scriptures is far more permanent than that.

Regarding the "iota" (Gk. ἰῶτα) or the "dot" (Gr. κεραία) that Jesus mentions, New Testament scholar Leon Morris explains:

> The iota was the smallest letter of the Greek alphabet, but here... it is generally understood to refer to the *yodh*, the smallest letter of the Hebrew alphabet... Jesus is saying, "Not the smallest letter, not the smallest part of a letter."[4]

It is, in other words, an emphatic affirmation of the validity of Scripture, and since biblical law is divinely inspired, it will endure (1 Tim. 3:15). As Rushdoony writes, "Until the end of time, the law

---

3. Nolland, NIGTC: *The Gospel of Matthew*, 218.
4. Leon Morris, PNTC: *The Gospel According to Matthew* (Grand Rapids, MI.: Eerdmans, 1992), 109-110.

of God, in its very detail, will remain. Its meaning and intent remain valid forever."[5]

From an apologetic standpoint to an emphatic assertion, the following verse continues with a stern warning—a exhortation from Jesus—that anyone who disregards one of the smallest commandments will be called "least in the kingdom of heaven." The contrast here is not between the rejection or acceptance of the entire law, applicable to both unbelievers and believers, as the commentator Lenski suggests. Instead, it implies that setting aside (as it says in the Greek) the least of the commandments, whether out of ignorance or selfishness, would mean misinterpreting or manipulating the meaning of a binding text and teaching others to do the same.[6] On the other hand, the one who both keeps and teaches the whole law will be called "great in the kingdom of heaven" because they are living out God's divine revelation—how biblical law should always be understood.

In verse twenty, Jesus' authority is asserted once again as He says, "I tell you", akin to a king addressing a subordinate or a judge speaking to

5. Rushdoony, *"Jesus and the Law"*.

6. Lenski, *The Interpretation of St. Matthew's Gospel* (Minneapolis, MN: Augsburg Publishing House, 1963), 211-212.

an accused. He declares that if one's righteousness does not "exceed that of the scribes and Pharisees," they will not enter the kingdom of God. During Jesus' earthly ministry, the scribes and Pharisees were regarded as the most pious among political-religious factions due to their rigorous study and teaching of the law (Luke 18:9-14). They held the highest status in Jewish society, and therefore, Jesus was stating that one must be far more righteous than these devout scribes and Pharisees, morally and culturally equated with "perfection." However, since achieving such stature is impossible for man, he cannot enter the kingdom of God on his own merits.[7] Jesus' words illustrate humanity's need for a saviour.

The motivation behind Jesus's apologetic statement and strong exhortation was to address "various antinomian tendencies," encompassing not only those who took a direct opposition to the law but also those who, "under the guise of obedience, contravened the spirit of the law."[8] In other words, external observance of the law without internal adherence contradicts the law,

---

7.   Craig L. Blomberg, *The New American Commentary: Matthew, Vol. 22* (Nashville, TN.: Broadman & Holman Publishers, 1992), 105.

8.   Ibid.

as illustrated in cases like hatred (Matt. 5:21-22) and adultery (Matt. 5:27-38). Despite this, antinomian perspectives have emerged and persisted as antitheses in the history and community of the Church.

The Same Law Applies

It is the isolation of this biblical text (Matt. 5:17-20) from its broader context within Matthean literature, including the rest of the biblical canon, that would lead to a misunderstanding of both the law and the gospel. For instance, in Matthew 7:12, Jesus taught what is known as the Golden Rule, "So whatever you wish that others would do to you, do also to them, for this is the Law and the Prophets." Is Jesus giving a new law that would abrogate the old ones? Far from it, as Nolland points out, "The Golden Rule not only summarizes Jesus' teaching but also summarizes the Law (and the Prophets)."[9]

Let us also consider John 13:34, which needs to be reconciled not only with the Johanine Gospel but with the collective Johanine literature (e.g., 1 John 5:2-3) and the entirety of Scripture. In this verse, where Jesus says, "A new command I give you: Love one another", it is not actually a "new"

---

9. Nolland, NIGTC: *The Gospel of Matthew*, 330.

command (Deut. 6:5; Lev. 19:18) that abolishes the old, but rather, as McQuilkin writes, "John used *kainos* [not *neos*], a new aspect of an old command." In Greek, *kainos* means a "new aspect, new depth, new fullness, or new scope."[10]

Therefore, the law was rejected only "as a mediator and as a source of justification," as Rushdoony expresses it. How can grace be understood without the law? And how can mercy and justice be interpreted if the law were to be abrogated?[11] Rushdoony's significant work, *Institutes of Biblical Law*, asserts the sovereignty of God over all things (Psalm 24:1) and because God created and owns everything, "true freedom can only be under God and His law."[12] As theologian R. C. Sproul explains, "We cannot live by our own law," true freedom can only be realized under the sovereignty of God (John 8:32).[13]

---

10. McQuilkin, *Understanding and Applying the Bible* (Chicago, IL.: Moody Publishers, 2009), 130.

11. Rushdoony, *The Institutes of Biblical Law* (Phillipsburg, NJ.: P&R Publishing), 7.

12. Boot, *The Mission of God: A Manifesto of Hope for Society* (Toronto, ON.: Ezra Press, 2016), 283.

13. R. C. Sproul, *Essential Truths of the Christian Faith* (Wheaton, IL.: Tyndale House, 1992), 17.

Jesus fully recognized the law, publicly affirmed it, and obeyed it. He came, "not as a destroyer or innovator, but to fulfill."[14] The text of Matthew 5:17-20 is clear in its meaning when reconciled with its historical, cultural, and homiletic context. Jesus explicitly declares that He did not come to abolish the law, to cancel it, or annul it, but to fulfill it, to enforce it, to enable His people to make the law an inward reality. As part of a larger homily, the King and Lawgiver announced the restoration of God's will and the inauguration of His kingdom, reaffirming the ethical demands of the Old Testament and confirming His teaching and authority with signs and wonders in the chapters to come.

Indeed, the kingdom of God is not without law in its nature; it is characterized by divine and just ethics established by God and enabled by the Holy Spirit. The law convicts people of their sins, restrains evil in the world, and guides believers in their progressive sanctification.

Van Til on the Law of God

While my response to the question "Is the Law of God still valid today?" has been answered in brief, there is still much to consider regarding its depth,

---

14. Ibid., 409.

scope, application, and meaning. As we seek to cultivate greater awareness and appreciation for God's law and its application in the Christian life, we have decided to publish what was once an un-published manuscript by Cornelius Van Til, *The Ten Commandments*. This foundational work by the father of presuppositionalism, grounded in our inherited Reformed Protestant tradition, informs us on how we should consider the law, both in contrast to the lawlessness of our world, and in its deeper meaning for our Christian life. It inspires us to righteousness and faith as we seek to glorify God as our supreme end. Van Til was, in many ways, a spiritual giant, a distinguished theologian, and an eloquent apologist and philosopher, so we have no doubt that this work, originally a syllabus for a course he taught at Westminster Theological Seminary will build you up in your devotion, discipleship, and on-going sanctification. If Van Til had a lasting influence on his students, such as Schaeffer, Frame, Rushdoony, Bahnsen, and many others, how much more does he have to teach us today? Personally, I am indebted to his writings, and I know that you will be too. May the teaching of the law be restored in the life of the Church, and may its goodness and beauty stand out in the life of the Christian in all ages (Psalm 1:1-2).

1

INTRODUCTION & PRESUPPOSITIONS

THE MAIN PRESUPPOSITION of the moral law is Christian theism. The one supreme question that appears momentarily when law is the subject of discussion is whether law is self-sufficient or whether it rests on absolute personality. The question put in this manner requires us to be either Biblical theists or Pragmatists. Law that does not rest in absolute personality must have originated from the space-time continuum of a self-sufficient universe and be for that reason sufficient unto itself. The issue between Christian theism and other thinking is not that of personality because that may mean no more than law is based on human personality or at least finite personality. The Scriptures contemplate the law as issuing from God as absolute personality.

As a corollary from this presupposition it follows that the whole of the temporal-spatial universe is created by God. The laws that are in this created universe are manifestations of the plan of God. The uniformity of nature about which science speaks so much exists not in independence of God but exists as an expression of a God of order. God is immanent in His creation. If one breaks a law of nature one breaks a law of God. Indifference to any law, whether that law be physical or normal, is an offense against God. To set law in opposition to God is like setting up a child in opposition to his father. That was the sin of Deism. On the other hand an absolute God cannot be identified with law in the temporal universe. John Fiske attempts to interpret the theology of Athanasius in this fashion in order to show that "Cosmic Theism" is really biblical theism. [1] If Fiske's interpretation were true absolute personality would have to be, though it cannot be, denied by theism. To identify law with God is to identify a child with its father. That was the sin of pantheism.

Again it follows from the theistic presupposition of an absolute God that law in history is expressive of a purpose of God. A deistic view of history once more involves an arbitrary separation

---

1.   *The Idea Of God.*

of God and laws in history to the destruction of both. On the other hand a pantheistic view of history involves an arbitrary identification of God and the laws of history to the destruction of both. Both Deism and Pantheism seek to elevate law but both destroy law in their attempt at elevation. Theism by elevating God has also elevated law. Neither Deism nor Pantheism can say that the breaking of law is an insult to God since both have identified law with God.

They must therefore say that the breaking of law is the breaking of God, i.e. the denial that God exists. When this is done the authority of law is gone and respectful law cannot long endure.

Absolute authority is therefore characteristic of and implied in the conception of law in the theistic sense. "The day thou eatest thereof thou shalt surely die," is not an arbitrary command. Any creature sinning against the law sinned against an absolute God and absolute separation from God naturally followed.

Thus also the condition of man's existence and of his realizing his destination is a complete fulfillment of the law of God on the part of man. Deism and Pantheism may say that it is advisable for man to be obedient to law since by so doing he will make more rapid progress than he would otherwise but only Theism can say that man destroys himself if he is disobedient to law. By thus tampering with law, Deism and Pantheism are playing with fire. More than that, in order to hold their relativistic views of law, they must first hold to a relativistic view of God; they play with fire and are themselves afire.

This leads us to the second presupposition of the moral law, namely the restorative and supplementative character of Christianity. Christianity wants to be restorative and supplementative of an original theism. Only in Christianity does man meet with an absolute God. With respect to the question of law this means that only Christian theism can speak of absolute law or law with absolute authority.

Christianity implies that man has by sin broken the law. He has therewith *ipso facto* destroyed the very condition of his existence and brought eternal punishment upon himself. Man became a Deist or a Pantheist. If man was to live at all, he had to be restored to respect for and obedience to law. Christ accomplished this restoration. Through His suffering He satisfies the penalty of the law. More than that, through His active and complete fulfillment of the law, He supplemented the original perfection of man so that those in Christ are heirs of eternal life without fail. Through His Word and Spirit, Christ has made "His own" partakers of His correct relationship to the law.

The knowledge of the law man must now receive from the Scriptures. Originally man found in experience the manifestation of, and the spontaneous response to, the law of God, but since the entrance of sin there had to be given an objective manifestation of, and a renewed response to, the law. Scripture as a concomitant to Christ gives the objective manifestation of absolute law and the Spirit of Christ gives to man the renewed subjective response when the law is seen. Only true Christians are true theists. Only true Christians know and obey the law.

To illustrate the point of the preceding paragraph we may contrast the Christian and Kantian conception of law. The reason for choosing Kant is that he is quite generally thought to have a greater respect for the absoluteness of the law than even a Christian could have. If Kant is found to be antitheistic most other philosophies will surely be such. First, then, as to the source of man's knowledge of the law, Kant looks "within" while the

Christian looks to the Scripture. Kant thinks that it is possible to come immediately into contact with absolute law while the Christian maintains that man, because now a sinner, must seek immediately to come into contact with absolute law. In other words Kant denies that sin has cut man loose from God and therefore also from a true knowledge of and respect for law. Accordingly Kant denies that Christianity is objectively and subjectively restorative of a true theism. The "radical evil" of Kant is not at all radical in comparison with the conception of sin as entertained by the Christian. Kant's radical evil is only a relative evil. That this is so is still more plain if in the second place we observe that Kant's refusal of a Biblical Epistemology as spoken of above involves and is based upon relativism in metaphysics. To seek for the solution of evil in experience because one regards it as an ineradicable and inherent ingredient in all possible experience, is to deny any Experience that is absolute. Evil is destructive of coherence and any absolute Experience must be completely coherent. Hence to say that evil is inherent in all possible experience is to deny the absoluteness of God and therefore the absoluteness of law. Thus the "*du sollst*" of Kant is reduced to the level of pragmatic advice. Only Christianity knows aught of an absolute law.

The preceding remarks may aid us to understand the inclusive sweep of the law as promulgated in the Scriptures. God addresses Himself to man generically, though directly to "His people" only. All men have disobeyed the law, yet all men must obey the law. The fact that the command comes directly to "God's people" only is due to the economy of redemption rather than to any difference of obligation between one nation and another. God deals with man generically and federally. Again, if it is true that as far as the essential demand of the law is concerned there is no difference between the believer and non-believer, it is, if possible, more true that the demand of God is the same for the people of God in all ages. The several stages in the economy of redemption do not in the least affect the requirements of God's law. The various stages of the economy of redemption in so far as they affect the law have to do only with the form of the law. During the old dispensation there was an emphasis on the external and national. During the new dispensation the emphasis is upon the internal and the universal. During the Old Testament the law was given in great externally. Many ceremonial

laws were elevated as far as the necessity of obedience is concerned, to an equality with the Ten
Commandments. On the other hand, this great
externalistic detail has disappeared since Christ's
appearance because with Him there is given to
His people a clearer and more central objective
revelation of God's law and a deeper and more
richly spiritual and therefore a more central subjective response to God's law. Thus in the new
dispensation it may become necessary, in order
to live up to the truly spiritual requirement of a
perfect obedience, to do away with many of the
external details of the Old Testament form of law.
Paul says it is a denial of the work of Christ to
cling to the Old Testament requirements after
Christ has come. The case is similar with respect
to the Old Testament nationalism. This nationalism is not an essential denial of the universal
sweep of the law. Hence the universalism of the
New Testament is not opposed to the nationalism of the Old Testament but is only a flowering
forth of it.

And if it is true that as far as the objective
manifestation of the law is concerned there is no
essential difference between the Old and the New
dispensation, this is equally true with the subjective response in each case. It is no more true of

the Old Testament than of the New that a mere external observance of the law was sufficient. The law of God is always spiritual and always requires love to God as the motive for its fulfillment. Hence also it is not true that obedience to the law was an Old Testament requirement, while in the New Testament love has been substituted for obedience. Obedience is love and love is obedience and they alone can adequately respond to a spiritual law.

The same point that there is no real difference between the people of Old and present day Christians in respect to the law of God can be further illustrated by pointing to the essential unity of the law and the gospel. There is a vast difference between them as far as the economy of redemption is concerned. Of this John speaks when he says that the law came by Moses but grace and truth by Jesus Christ. But the very content of the Gospel is that Christ has fulfilled the law. Thus the joy of the gospel is that man can in Christ know and obey the law and therefore live in the presence of God forever. There is no Gospel but that of the law. On the other hand, the Gospel is law because all must obey it. In answer to the question of the Jews as to what they must do in order to work the works of God Jesus replies that they must believe on the name of the Son of God.

Still further, if there is no essential but only an economical difference between the promulgation of and response to the law in the Old and in the New dispensations, it follows that the form in which the law may come cannot be used as an argument for or against the validity of the law. The form of the Old Testament propagation of the law was necessarily externalist and temporalist. The promises and the threats, for instance, pertained to things in this life. A long life in Canaan under the vine and fig tree constituted the substance of the promise while bodily death was the substance of the punishment under the Old dispensation.

But this fact did not make the law less spiritual. Canaan here below was, as Abraham saw, prophetic of the Canaan hereafter, and physical death is, for a sinner not reconciled, the gateway to external death. It will not do to deny universal and permanent significance to the commandment that promises to children a long and earthly life if they are obedient to parents on the ground that that is manifestly an Old and not a New Testament promise. The fulfillment of that promise may not come in a same manner now as it once did, but the fulfillment is no less real or certain.

One further point must be mentioned as to the form of the law as given in the Old Testament, and that is that the law constantly says, "thou shalt not," instead of, "thou shalt." Why this negative form? To answer this question we should recall the general character of Christianity as restorative of an original theism. Originally there was no reason for this negative emphasis. Man spontaneously obeyed the law and in so far as there was occasion for God to add commandments by direct communication to that which was given to man by nature, the positive and the negative forms of giving such commandments could be evenly balanced. But with the entrance of sin man constantly evaded and broke God's law. Moreover, his ignorance of the true law increased. Hence if God was to bring His law into the knowledge and obedience of man, He had to say more often what man should *not* do than what he should do. The child, because he is a sinful child, will attempt to be a law unto himself. It is impossible then that parents should not more often say "do not" than "do."

Yet this fact should not blind us to the truth that it is positive obedience, positive accomplishment of good, and not only a negative refraining from evil that God desires. It is accordingly necessary that we make this positive demand of God's law our starting point. We shall ask in the case of each commandment what it is that God wants of man in order to use that as a standard by which to judge how far man has fallen short of fulfilling this demand.

As to method, that is the opposite of that of the modern philosophy and psychology of religion schools. They work on the assumption that evil is as basic as the good in man and the universe. Hence they would simply trace the road by which man has, with the aid of law, enabled himself to escape somewhat from the complete control of evil. From their point of view it is the height of dogmatism to presuppose the evil in this universe is due to a human deflection from an absolute God. We, on the other hand, maintain that unless this is true there is no law at all and all morality lacks foundation. Hence we cannot do otherwise than follow the path demanded by the central presupposition of theism.

1.1   The Moral Law

Before beginning the discussion of the First Commandment we must clearly have in mind not only what is meant by law in general but what is meant by the moral law. We have purposely made no distinction between kinds of law up to this point in order to call attention to the fact that a theist regards all law differently than a non-theist. Even physical or natural law means something quite different for a Christian theist than it does for an anti-theist. According to theism, man lives and moves and has his being in an atmosphere of the law of God both for his body and for his soul. To live in this atmosphere meant his freedom as it means freedom to a fish to live in its native element. But when man broke the law at one point he broke it at every point. The moral and the physical are inextricably interwoven. As prophet, priest and king, man was to know, to dedicate to God, and rule over for God the whole of the physical universe. When through sin he became a prophet without a mantle, a priest without a sacrifice, and a king without a crown, he brought his body along with his soul and the universe around him along with his body into ruin. On the other hand, with Christ the physical world, as well as the body of man, and the body of man as well as his soul, are restored to their normal relationships to the law of God.

By this way of conceiving the relationship of the physical and the moral we stand again in opposition to antitheistic thought which assumes that there is no connection between the physical and the moral. In all discussions on responsibility by non-theistic writers, man is, as far as physical law is concerned, either a child of fortune or of misfortune, and no more. It is considered to be obviously ludicrous to think of mankind as in any way responsible for famine or pestilence. But again, we cannot do otherwise than hold to our view since it is part of Christian theism and Christian theism seems to us the most reasonable philosophy of life to hold.

1.2 Physical and Moral Law

Holding then to the close connection between, and the common origin and authority of both physical and moral law, we may nevertheless distinguish between them. Physical law is the ordinance of God for non-responsible creation.

Moral law is the ordinance of God for His reasonable creatures. In the case of physical law God does not expect, while in the case of moral law He does expect, a self-conscious response. To the extent then that man is capable by virtue of his creation in the image of God to react self-consciously in any direction to the law of God, man acts morally. By acting morally, we only signify in this instance that he acts self-consciously upon the law of God. We cannot even say that he acts morally only when concerned with matters of obligation while in intellectual matters morality does not enter. Man ought to think right, that is, be a true prophet; man ought to do right; that is, be a true king; and man ought to feel right, that is, be a true priest. In the broadest sense of the term then, all self-conscious response to the law of God, wherever revealed, is moral action. When the term moral is used its opposite is non-moral.

1.3   The Moral and the Religious

For man, as a self-conscious and so morally acting being, there were two main spheres of self-conscious response in which he might obey the law of God. There was an aspect of the general law of God for man that pertained more directly to man's relation to God. There was a second aspect of the general law of God for man that pertained more directly to man's relation to his fellow man. These aspects overlap to be sure since in the ultimate sense all law is the law of God, but there is a relative distinction between them. When man obeyed the first aspect of the law he was truly religious and when he broke this first aspect of the law he was irreligious or falsely religious. When man obeyed the second aspect of the law he was moral in the narrower sense of the term and when man disobeyed the second aspect of the law he was immoral,[2] in the narrower sense of the term. When, in common parlance, we speak of an irreligious man, that is one who does not attend to devotions, we do not say that he is also an immoral man, that is, that he cannot be a good father and neighbor. On the other hand, Scripture and experience afford numerous illustrations of those that said a gift by which father or mother might have profited was *corban*, dedicated to the Lord. The truly moral man must also be the truly religious man and the truly religious man must also be the truly moral man. An immoral man, however much he seems to be religious, is really irreligious, only he sins less directly against God than he who openly breaks God's law in so far as it pertains directly to man's relation to God.

When we now have these distinctions in mind and we look at the Decalogue or "moral" law, we see that the first three commandments deal chiefly with religion.

---

2. Even so we do not use immoral in the still narrower sense when it signifies an addiction to a special kind of sin.

For this reason they are not strictly commandments with respect to morality. Yet they are parts of the moral law in the wider sense of the term since in the Law, God comes to man as a self-conscious being. Secondly, we notice that the sixth to ninth commandments deal quite definitely with the norms of man's relation to his fellow man. But again, this does not imply that the breaking of any one or all of these laws does not affect your religious standing. The unity of the law, in its religious and more definitely moral aspects must ever be kept in view. The fourth and fifth commandments are of a mixed character, indicating the close unity between the religious and the moral, while the tenth clearly shows that one and the same motive produces true religion and true morality.

How contrary this way of connecting the religious and the moral is to the modern temper may be seen from an article by W. E. Pitkin in the *Century Magazine* of Oct. 1926, on, "Our Moral Anarchy." Out of five hundred educated people who replied to a questionnaire about the relative value of the various commandments of the decalogue no less than one hundred and two reported that "they could not deal with the first four commandments because in their opinion these have no moral value whatsoever." [3] Then there was a large group who would, in some sense, deal with both tables of the law but would at least make the second table of the law come first. As an example of these he speaks of the Modernists. Of them he says: "What Jesus placed first the modernist places second; and what Jesus placed second the modernist places first." [4] Add to these the moral communists who profess not to care about the first table of the law at all and Pitkin's statement that there are five moral modernists, and two socialists for every moral fundamentalist, and it becomes apparent that as Christian ministers we should stress the irreligiousness of religion without morality and stress still more the immorality of morality without religion.

It will not be possible to attempt to trace the various manifestations of the general autonomic morality about us today. [5] Still less will it be feasible to seek for the reasons that bring about morality that as theists we cannot but be sorry to see. The task of the minister of the gospel is to do this first of all. But that is not the end of his task. He must preach the full demand of the law

3.   p. 643.

4.   p. 645.

5.   Cf. W. Lippmann, *Preface to Morals*.

to love God above all and one's neighbor as one's self. How sadly the pulpit has neglected its task in this respect. There are many who make a dash into the law to defend the eighteenth amendment or something else that draws their attention. But what good will that do if the congregation has not been nurtured upon the preaching of the law in the sense of placing before men their whole duty with respect to God and man. "To the law and to the testimony if they speak not according to this word, surely there is no morning for them" (Isa. 8:20).

2

THE FIRST COMMANDMENT: RELIGION

2.1 Remarks

A FULL DISCUSSION of the commandment would require an exposition of the origin and nature of religion. We only discussed the nature of religion and not the question of origin. The question of origin of religion does not come up because theism is the presupposition of the decalogue.

In second place, we note that the answer one gives to the question of the nature of religion is also determined by one's theistic position. According to theism man is inherently religious. But there are many today who will admit this fact and yet are not theists.[1] Their reason for such a

---

1. Cf. Any of the idealistic writers on the history and philosophy of religion or many modernist preach-

view is the fact that history and psychology have not been able to find any irreligious stage in man's development. Yet at the back of history there is placed the mysterious void. And this void changes the nature of religion. At most, religion becomes a vague reverence for the Mysterious.[2] Christian theism, on the other hand, presupposes God at the back of history. Thus a reasonable foundation is given to religion. Thus the nature of religion is determined by this foundation of God.

Then further it is involved in theism that man originally had the true religion. Again there are many non-theists who will admit this contention. They hold all religions to be true religions. But the theist holds only Christianity to be the true religion. The other religions are deflections from an original theism.

We mention this fact because it is quite common today to talk about religion as though it is altogether possible to determine the nature of religion without bringing in any metaphysical discussion. It is said to be a matter for psychology alone. That such a position is untenable is once apparent if it be remembered that religion deals

---

ers such as Dr. Fosdick.

2. Cf. Carlyle, *Heroes and Heroworship*.

with the Unseen. What about the Unseen? No full answer can be given by psychology.[3] We find it to be a fact then that some sort of metaphysics is always involved in our study of the nature of religion. The so-called scientific method of determining the nature of religion differs from the theistic method in as much as the "scientific method" has assumed a pragmatic relativistic metaphysics.

Others will admit that metaphysics is involved in the determination of the essence of religion but are bound to be "scientific" in the method by which they establish their metaphysics. Dr. Harry Emerson Fosdick may serve as an illustration of this way of dealing with the nature of religion. In a sermon preached Nov. 9, 1930, he spoke of man's relation to the Unseen. He warned against trusting those who claim to know all about the Unseen either positively or negatively. The Unseen is uncertain. Yet we may be confident toward it. Every new revelation that has come to us from the Unseen shows it to be more wonderful than before. This position is said to be Biblical. In proof of the contention that the Unseen is to us uncertain, Christ's words: "My God, my God, why hast thou forsaken me," were quoted among others.

---

3. Eddington, *Science and the Unseen World*.

Now it would seem plain that such a sermon is neither Christian nor theistic. Without justification it is assumed that Christ is no more than a human personality instead of a divine personality which has assumed human nature. Without justification it is assumed that there is no absolute God for whom the unseen is an open book. If God is what theism holds him to be, an absolute personality, pure religion is determined by man's relationship to God instead of to the Unseen in general. The point in dispute between Modernism and theism is the absoluteness of God; a finite deity, or polytheism is all that Modernism can allow for. At first sight it appears to be very scientific to base reference to the unknown exclusively upon the "facts." But when the arguments based upon these "facts" must presuppose a complete metaphysical relativism for their cogency the scientific character of such arguments suffers greatly. We protest not against the acceptance of relativism or the presupposition of it, if only it be plainly stated how this differs from Christianity and traditional theism. If that were done the "common people" would not be misguided by terminology that sounded Christian. If that were done less of the *"intelligentsia"* would be led astray because they would then see the consequences of their choice.

2.2   What is Commanded

2.2.1   *Religion for Adam*

The law we have was promulgated after the entrance of sin. Originally there was no need of such an external promulgation. Adam was spontaneously religious. The law was written on his heart. The prophet Jeremiah promised that the Messiah would in principle restore this condition. Christ has given us once more the true love for God and therefore also the true love for God's law.

When the law as we know it says, "Thou shalt, etc."...it does directly address the Israelitish man, and no one else. Yet since in Israel's history the redemptive principle is operative, generic man is not excluded but definitely included in the term, "thou."

So we may conclude also with respect to all that is commanded in the various commandments that even without the necessity of any commandment man's relation to God was once what it is here contemplated in the law.

In order now to ascertain what true religion was in Paradise we must recall that man was created as prophet, priest and king. As a prophet man had to think God's thought after him. Here lies the realm of intellect and of truth or science. As a priest man was to dedicate himself and the whole creation to God. Here is the realm of emotions, and of aesthetics or art. As a king man was to reign over the whole creation in God's stead. Here is the realm of the will and of action. But the intellect, the emotions and the will are but aspects of one central ego, the human personality. Now it is this central ego that is placed face to face with the absolute personality of God in the first commandment. In the commandments that follow, man will be told about the various ways and methods by which and through which he may be truly religious in morality, but in this commandment, man in the inmost holy of holies of his being is placed directly face to face with God. The relation of man's heart to God is all that really matters. If this relation is sound, all else is well. If this relation is false, all else is false. The truly religious man is the truly moral man. In preaching on this commandment we should bring in nothing else but this inner relationship of man's soul to God.

Behold, the Lord thy God is God alone. That was an ever returning refrain that came to Israel.

Only when man has fallen into inconceivable depths of sin is it possible that he should ever think of other gods. Polytheism is not a natural stepping stone towards theism but a sad deflection from it.

This point becomes still more clear if we note that only man was created in God's image. Only man can be religious. Religion involves a relation between two personalities. Religion is always a covenant affair. Only from a self-conscious being like himself could God receive religious adoration. How far much of modern research has drifted from this position may be noted if one recalls how some evolutionists have thought that they observed religion in animals. This extreme position is no longer commonly held. Yet, almost without exception, the leading schools of the philosophy of religion hold that morality has historically descended from the non-moral and religion from the non-religious. Now this viewpoint implicitly, if not explicitly, denies not only the creation of man in God's image but denies God Himself. If God does exist then man is created in His image, since in that case no self-conscious personality could originate from any other source. On the other hand, if self-conscious finite personality exists, God exists as its creator since finite personality can find its explanation in nothing but in God. At any rate, if religion has derived from the non-religious then its essence is fully expressed in loyalty to vague principles of goodness, truth and beauty instead of reverence for an absolute God, since the Universe is in that case a wider concept than God.

We are now prepared to see what religion is on the basis of Christian theism. Man's intellect was to be fixed upon God. In God man would find an inexhaustible depth of knowledge. Thus and thus only could man have genuine knowledge and be a true prophet. Secondly, true religion involves a fixing of our desires upon God, an earnest striving after communion with Him, a possession of Him in our souls. This is true mysticism. Thirdly, true religion implies the entire submission of our will to God. God's will for man is not to be felt by man as a burden to him. It is rather to be considered as the chief source of joy for man.

These three elements together constitute true religion. They imply faith in God, love of God, trust in God. This is sometimes called "godliness," sometimes "fear of God," and sometimes "love of God."

2.2.2   *Religion after the Entrance of Sin*

There is a large element of truth in the claim of recent philosophy that religion is at bottom the same. It could not be otherwise. False religion must be an imitation of true religion. Man has no resources but those derived from God. There is not a speck of originality in man apart from originality that implicates into the revelation of God. Thus theism and anti-theism are agreed on this point. Yet their agreement is formal and no more. The non-theist maintains that religions are essentially the same because theism is but a bit higher than other religions. Theism maintains that religions are similar in form because other religions are an imitative deflection from an original theism. Due to the operation of God's common grace, these false religions have been able to come to a great degree of similarity to Christian theism. Once these points are clearly understood, that theism is original and that the principle of common grace has enabled sinful man to develop a pseudo-religion that greatly resembles true religion, it will keep us from confusion. On the one hand, there has often been an underestimation of pagan religions on the part of orthodox Christians. There is some truth in the charge made again and again that orthodox Christians have sought to defend the truth of their religion by an artificial isolation. [4] It is very true that such a policy is self-destructive. Christianity is theism come to its own. We desire the widest possible foundation for Christianity. "Recreation", i.e. redemption, is based upon and is restorative of creation. In the right sense of the word, Christianity is as old as creation or at least as old as the *protoevangelium*. It cannot be too oft reiterated that Christianity introduces nothing new but that it reintroduces the old. On the other hand, there is a tendency to obliterate the distinction between Christian and pagan religion. Their formal similarity has led many a writer to see no more than a difference of quantity between them. Now, we expect this from avowed non-theists. But there is also much valueness on this matter on the part of professing Christian theists. Christianity is said to stand in a climactic relation to the other religions. So the author of "Christ of the Indian Road" seems to conceive of the matter. Now, this way of putting the matter is ambiguous. It is the truth and yet not the whole truth. Christ is "the desire of the nations" but in what sense? In the sense that

---

4.   A. C. Knudson recently charged us with this. *Vide,* *Doctrine of God.*

they are seeking for just this sort of reality? If this were true, Paul's statement that the "natural man" is "at enmity" against God must be revised. But since we take Scripture to be consistent with itself, we can see in "the desire" of the nations, in their truth-seeking aspirations, no more than a vague sense of lack. As far as their self-conscious and purposive action is concerned, they have definitely turned their backs on God. They are apostate from God. Either this is true because theism is true or this is not true because theism is not true. Yet as the prodigal of Christ's parable, they sometimes feel that they are seeking to satisfy their needs with the husks of antitheism. They sometimes even build an altar to the "unknown God." But even when an apostle comes direct from this unknown God to them in order to make Him known, they answer that he speaks "foolishness." Only when it pleases the Spirit to "save through the foolishness of preaching those that believe," will they accept this God for whom they have so long been "seeking."

We conclude then that in order to give to Christianity its broadest basis as in truth the religion of man, we must beware of false isolation. On the other hand, in order to preserve Christianity so that it may be seen to be the religion of man, we must not fear to maintain for it a true isolation. A false isolation could permanently retain the hot-bed stage of Christianity preventing its taking root in the open fields of humanity and bearing fruitage for the race. A true isolation weeds out thorns and briars that would choke the plant once it flourishes in the open field. By the truly Biblical doctrine of common grace we are saved from the danger of undue underestimation or undue overestimation of the religion and morality of paganism.

The phraseology employed by the theology of the church may help us to distinguish clearly with respect to the matter in hand. The best tradition of the Church has sought to give expression, on the one hand, to Paul's picture of man's total depravity, and on the other hand, to Paul's picture of the heathen as accusing or excusing themselves according to the standard of an internal moral law.

Clearly then, Christianity is qualitatively distinct from Paganism. There is no other name given by which men may be saved for eternity than the name of Jesus. The natural man can do no spiritual good. But equally clear is it that the natural man has not yet run the full gamut of wickedness. The germs of every sin are within. A Nero may develop into a veritable devil while still on earth but most men do not. By the Spirit's operation in common grace they are temporarily restrained from developing the full measure of the evil inherent in them.

Hence they can do things that are of service for a tolerable life on earth; they can do the morally good. This distinction between the spiritual and the morally good is not wholly unambiguous since in another connection it was pointed out that to be truly moral one must also be truly religious. In this connection, the terms are contrasted and may be so used in order to indicate as clearly as possible that the "relatively good" in the "absolutely evil" is of value for this life but not for eternity.

2.2.3 Religion after the Entrance of the Redemptive Principle

Religions became true religion in principle once more after the redemptive power became active in the world. We should emphasize the word *principle*. It calls mention to the fact that religion is not yet perfect in degree. This will be the case in heaven. But the Scriptures do not hesitate to speak of the redeemed as altogether holy, altogether righteous. A deep antithesis exists between the redeemed on this earth. This deep antithesis will finally be "a great gulf fixed" in the hereafter. The redeemed, in whom the life that they now live is the life of Christ, say from the depth of their heart: "Oh, how love I thy law, it is my meditation night and day."

We must observe again that this holds for all the "Israel of God," including the Israel of the Old Testament. The true children of Abraham are they who believe in the Messiah whose external and temporal relationship to Abraham is internalized and externalized in Christ.

It is of great significance for a believer to understand his relationship to the law of God. God has made a covenant of works with man. This covenant signifies that those that fully satisfy the law of God and consequently are perfect as their Father in heaven is perfect will have eternal life. On the other hand, those who have not satisfied the law of God will have eternal death. We may see two men walking together, both in rosy health apparently. Forty years after we see one of them come to old age. The other has long since died. Already when we saw the two at first, the one had the germs of the disease working in his body though he seemed to be as healthy as the other. Similarly two men may offhand appear to be morally equally healthy. Yet the one is "right with God" and therefore lives and will live while the other is not right with God and though he seems to live is really dead.

In order to understand this difference between the two classes of men we must see clearly what Christ's work has been with respect to the law. Now, Christ has negatively, by his passive obedience, removed for those in Him the curse and penalty of the law. That is, those in Christ are no longer guilty before God but righteous. Hence they cannot come into judgment. The wrath of God against sin has spent itself upon Him who became sin for us. Thus we are "covered" from the "wrath to come." It is this that as ministers of Christ we may bring to those that are facing death. Few Christians today seem to experience the unspeakable comfort that comes from the assurance that Christ's righteousness is ours. Most Christians desire to cleanse and purify to some extent the "filthy rags" of their own righteousness. Their constant effort to get to heaven by the golden rule gives them not a moment of peace. The threat of God: "Cursed is every one that doeth not the law of God" hangs over everyone that seeks without Christ or merely by his assistance to fulfill the law of God. On the other hand, perfect freedom from fear of judgment comes into the hearts of those who trust in Christ's righteousness alone.

The second aspect of the work of Christ with respect to the law is that by His active obedience He merits heaven for us. He fulfills the requirement of the covenant of works, that man should obey perfectly and thereupon enter heaven. Thus all those in Christ are not only relieved from the curse but have the promise of eternal life. We are heirs of God and joint-heirs with Christ.

If now the work of Christ with respect to the law is clear, we must note specifically that Christ has done the same thing for the Old Testament believer that He did for the new. There is no essential difference between an Old Testament believer and a New Testament believer as far as the law is concerned. For both Christ has borne the penalty of the law. For both Christ has merited heaven. For neither was the law a way by which he himself could earn freedom from the curse and an entrance into the promised land. For neither was the law meant to be a way to life independently of Christ. For both was the law given as a regulator of a life of gratitude for redemption received.

Readily granted as these matters are with respect to New Testament believers, they are not so readily apparent with respect to the Old

Testament believer. Paul, in the Epistle to the Galatians, seems to make a very great distinction between the two dispensations as regards the relation of the believer to the law in each case. But however great he makes the distinction he does not for a moment forget the still greater distinction between those who seek by their own righteousness to inherit life and those who seek salvation through the righteousness of Christ alone. In fact, Paul's distinction between the Old and New Testament dispensation of the law is made explicitly in the interest of deepening the gulf between the righteousness of God and the righteousness of man. His very point in the argument against the Judaizer was that unless they interpreted the Old Testament purpose of the law spiritually, and therewith realize that true righteousness was, even for the Old Testament believer, accomplished by Christ, they would be classed with those who seek by their own righteousness to enter heaven. Paul had himself experienced that to attempt to scale heaven by the works of the law is like trying to carry water in a sieve. Hence he seeks definitely to prove that not even in the Old Testament were men taught to seek by works to merit life. Once sin has entered, man can enter heaven by the covenant of grace alone. And this covenant of grace is not made of none effect. Paul tells us, by the law, that is, as given to Moses, that came in afterwards. That law itself is subsidiary to the covenant of grace. Its stringency and irrevocable nature which appeared so awfully under the dispensation "of condemnation," was calculated to compel men to seek salvation by grace. Thus the law was to be a taskmaster to Christ. Thus the law said, "Salvation is in me, but only in the Christ."

So we see that we can still preach the law in the same twofold sense that it had for Israel. In the first place the demands of God upon men are as absolute as ever, and man is as unable to meet these demands as ever. Thus I may learn, "how great my sins and miseries are," and the law becomes for me the "taskmaster leading to Christ." In the second place when I have felt my guilt and impotence with respect to the law of God and have fled to Christ for refuge, I may learn from the law in all its detail how I may regulate my life of gratitude for redemption received.

In both these respects it is highly necessary to preach the law today. Much confusion reigns on the first point. It is quite often said that everybody can learn from experience the misery of men. We need only point to hospitals to convince men of the need of Christ. Or, if this is not sufficient, at least the conscience in man condemns him sufficiently to make him realize the need of a Redeemer. Yet no one's conscience and no one's experience has ever, apart from the law as found in Scripture, told him that he is worthy of eternal punishment. Experience, just because it is sinful experience, cannot love the law of God. Experience, because it is sinful experience, is at enmity against God. Hence it will not even admit that there is any such thing as a law that is absolute because it is fixed by an absolute God. Experience, because it is sinful experience, seeks to be a law unto itself and does not feel guilty before God but at best guilty before itself because of the transgression of law. Consequently there is no sorrow "toward God," that leads to repentance; experience as such cannot be the taskmaster to Christ. We cannot omit the preaching of the law as the source, the only source of our knowledge of sin.

Then, as to the preaching of the law as the regulator of the believer's life, we may say that this too has been neglected. And again our ready emphasis upon experience as a teacher is at fault. True, when experience is "Christian" experience, it should no longer be contrasted to the law because in this case it has developed in connection with law. But this exactly is the point. We tend so easily to separate experience from law. And this is fatal to experience. Conscience as such is not "the voice of God," only a "Christian" conscience is and that only indirectly. Even the Christian conscience must constantly be recharged. It "runs out" so easily. In the first place, its field of vision narrows so easily. Many things are not known by it to be sin unless the law did so speak of it. But God's law is "very wide." In the second place, conscience alone loses its sensitiveness. But the law enters into the recesses of the heart. Deeper by far does it descend into man's being than Freud's psychology. The torch of human psychology leaves the depths of the human heart as a frozen marsh while the Sun of God's law thaws the marsh bringing into movement the many scorpions, adders, and poisonous insects. Thus the law when seen to be "spiritual" makes us yearn for purity, for relief from the pollution of sin as it once made us cry out for relief from its guilt. The Christian who seeks to guide his life carefully by the law of God is always conscious of breaking the law. The Christian in name, on the contrary, will readily say: "all these things have I kept from my youth up."

We may note in passing that if the law is thus preached in all its spirituality it will serve as a better cure for social ills than the much-praised education of our day. The Socratic dictum that knowledge is virtue, that is, that men will do the law if they only see it, has led men to propagate the idea that education as such will make men good. But education as such cannot enable men to see the spirituality of the law. To see that spirituality man must be regenerated. "Regeneration plus education" instead of "education alone" should be our slogan.

2.3   What is Forbidden

The substitution of "other gods" for the true God, we have seen, is the substance of false religions. "For that they exchanged the truth of God for a lie, and worshipped and served the creature rather than the Creator, who is blessed forever" (Rom 1:25). A greater subversion cannot be conceived. Man, especially, but also the whole creation is made the object of worship. How radically different the modern interpretation of pagan religion is. According to it, man was groping for the true God, but while on his way quite incidentally, as an aid to his faith, worshipped sun, moon and stars. According to this interpretation, the non-moral precedes the moral and it is on this point that the battle between the two forms of interpretation must chiefly be fought.

We hold that to make religion derive from the non-moral kills not only all religion and morality but all human experience in general since it surrounds man with a meaningless void. To maintain the Biblical doctrine of an original perfection of man is therefore not only to cling to an "external authority" or to "mere tradition" but it is at the same time to cling to theism.

Now, the facts of a pagan religion are in harmony with our theistic conception of religion. There is a qualitative difference between any and all the religions of paganism and the religion of theism as found in Christianity. No matter how close the formal resemblance to Christianity may be, pagan religion always worships the creature, while Christianity worships God.

It does not follow from this that there are no gradations among the pagan religions so that all of them should be equally valueless. The doctrine of common grace allows us to make much difference between the one and the other, while the doctrine of special grace forbids us ever to wipe out the qualitative distinction that separates all of them from Christianity. The very difference between these religions is due to widely differing measures of God's common grace. Through common grace civilization has gradually advanced so that man has been enabled solely to rid himself of some of the more sensuous forms of creature worship. But creature worship, even the most refined form of non-Christian religion, remains. Even when he worships *á la modernisme* the ideals of the good, the true and the beautiful it is still creature worship since these ideals are not conceived of as posited by God.

We must now briefly survey the chief forms of anti-theistic religion.

2.3.1 Atheism

Atheism is the most defiant and open denial of the very existence of God. In it the principle of sin has reached its climax. Even so, man cannot wholly rid himself of the idea of God. The atheist's very fighting against God may be an indication of dread of God. There is much of the bravado spirit in the movement. This bravado spirit can only temporarily be maintained. In hell there will be no atheists. It will be impossible to deny God's existence at the judgment day and after.

Atheism is worse than paganism. Paganism at least serves gods. It admits something of its insufficiency; it indicates some desire to get in touch with higher powers. Atheism, on the other hand has hermetically sealed itself against God. The issue will have to be decided by a test of strength alone.

There is much practical atheism in every civilized land. The reign of law has caused many to say in effect if not in words, "The Lord will not do good, neither will he do evil" (Zeph. 1:12). Religion has become for many a side-issue in life. God is no longer thought of as controlling and affecting our lives every moment in every respect through every possible avenue. In view of this fact, it is necessary to preach the prophetic message that the Lord "will punish the men that are settled on this land, that say in their heart, the Lord will not do good, neither will he do evil." The picture of the judgment day is nowhere more terrible than when set before those who ignore Yahweh. To be ignored is almost as great an insult as to be openly defied. Perhaps it may even be counted a greater insult inasmuch as an open defiance at least "figures with" God, giving him credit for some power.

2.3.2 *Nature religions*

Man, though having declared his independence, still has to live as the prodigal on the substance of the father. Moreover, he feels something of the absurdity of having elevated himself to the position of God. Later in history he will openly declare his moral autonomy (Kant). For the present he must look about him for some object of worship. He finds these objects in the lower creation. The lower creation affects him in many ways and that beyond his own control. Man is as a child that has brought a kettle of hot water down upon itself and blames the kettle for his misery. Man only seeks escape from the evil consequences of sin as they face him in the various powers of destruction. Instead of realizing that the powers of destruction are agencies of God so that he ought to go *to* God to find relief from them, man defies these agencies and worships them. The stupidity and futility of sin are therewith fully and typically illustrated.

1. The lower forms of nature-religion really do not have any gods but only souls. Animism and fetishism are illustrations this type.

2. The higher forms of nature worship do have gods. Creative imagination has entered in to create sculpture and mythology.

(a) The Semitic forms of the higher nature religions have developed some sort of transcendence idea. Sin has brought God into His creation and therewith denied God's transcendence above His creation. In this respect the whole emphasis on the immanence of God in modern theology is a plain and extreme form of the transgression of the first commandment. Yet at different times and in different degrees man has felt that he needs a transcendent God. Not as though he has of himself come to any true transcendence idea. Such a true transcendence idea could only come to him again by revelation from God; and that not by revelation through human experience as such since human experience as such is sinful. Transcendence as conceived of by non-theistic thought is separation. This is deism.

(b) The Indo-Germanic forms of higher nature religions have stressed the need of the nearness of God. They speak much of the father and son relationship. But again, the true immanence idea is perverted till it means identity. This is pantheism.

Thus the pendulum-swing of antitheistic religion has been that from deism to pantheism. And philosophy motivated by the same antitheistic principle has run through a similar course.

It should be noted that corresponding to the false object in religion, antitheistic man has cherished an equally false subjective attitude. There is nothing of the true service of the heart to be found. As a false prophet man seeks to interpret the Universe without reference to God. The evil powers are assumed to exist as powers independent of God. Man will not be "taught of God." He has lost his reactivity of mind. As a false king he seeks to rule over nature for his own interest alone. Nature, science, art and government, all of them by turn are made man's servants without also being made God's servants. Man will not rule in God's stead. He will receive no orders but only give them. He has lost obedience.

As a false priest he dedicates all things to himself instead of offering all things to God. That which would serve God he keeps from serving God. His heart is estranged from God and shuns God altogether or seeks a false familiarity. Man prays to the gods but not to God.

He prays for relief but not forgiveness. If he has remorse, it is not a "sorrow towards God," but a sorrow that evil has come due to one's own folly.

2.3.3 *Ethical Religions*

The ethical religions are higher than the nature-religions and approach more nearly in form to theism. In the first place they are monotheistic. Consequently God is represented as not only controlling the natural but also as controlling the moral world order. Secondly, these religions believe in a revelation from God in the form of sacred scriptures, Brahmanism has its Vedas, Buddhism its Pittakas, Confucianism its Kings, Parzism its Avesta and Mohammedanism its Koran. Yet in no case is the moral law conceived as proceeding with inviolable authority from an absolute God. And as to subjective religion we do not find that godliness which blends a true sense of exaltation and of proximity of God. If it be remembered that in the first commandments God places himself squarely before the center of man's personality requiring of man that he look nowhere else for his joy and peace, it is readily seen that all of these religions are sad deflections from theism.

Going out to the nations to bring the gospel of Christianity means more than spreading the knowledge of civilization or of a higher ethical mode of life. It means rather to bring to men the knowledge of the requirements of a holy and righteous God who can in no sense tolerate sin, but who in His condescending love will forgive sin in Christ in order to make men true prophets, priests, and kings again. Once they know this

God in Christ, they will not worship nature but nature's God, they will not worship law but the God of law.

But would that idolatry were prevalent in pagan countries alone. The first commandment as the foundation of all the rest needs to be preached in this country, and in all civilized countries as well as in pagan lands.

3

THE SECOND COMMANDMENT: WORSHIP

3.1 Remarks

THE FIRST COMMANDMENT deals with religion proper as the foundation of morality. The second commandment deals with the external expression of religion. The first commandment teaches us that we must serve God; the second how we can do this correctly as far as the external expression of religion is concerned. Thus these two commandments relate to altogether distinct matters. This is quite easily forgotten. One sometimes hears a sermon on the first commandment in which all manner of material that deals with images of God is brought. Yet when men use images in worship they are not necessarily seeking to substitute a false for the true God. It may be a defective worship of the true God. True, a transgression of the second commandment leads very easily to a transgression of the first. Images very easily attract exclusive attention to themselves and thus become objects instead of means of worship. Yet it will not do to identify image worship with idolatry. If we may make comparison at all between various commandments of the law the first commandment is more central than any other objectively and therefore also more central than the second. Once a substitution is made for the one true God, all true religion and morality at once disappears.

3.2   What is Commanded

To ascertain what the positive content of the second commandment is, it is first of all necessary that we form a truly Biblical conception of what is meant by the image of God. Now, we can speak of the image of God in the sense of the idea that God has of Himself. God alone knows His own being. He alone has the complete and true image of Himself. This conception of the image of God is one of the factors that enters into religion and also into worship. No true religion or true worship is possible unless God reveals to man, according to man's capacity, something of His image of Himself. All non-theistic religion and worship attempts in vain to do without this self-revelation of God. It begins by analyzing man. Now, it is important to be sure in order to form a true conception of worship to know what man is. But how can one know what man is unless one knows what God is? The nature of man, and therefore the nature of true religion and true worship in so far as it is determined by the nature of man, is determined by the nature of God.

Hence, when we speak of the image of God in the second sense of the term meaning thereby the image of God in man, we have the second and also secondary determining factor in the makeup of religion and worship. By the image of God in man we do not signify the idea that man may have formed of God. It is not "my idea of God," but "God's idea of me" that we are after. That is, we must know man's makeup as he was formed of God. As such, we may distinguish between God's image in man in the wider and in the narrower sense of the term. By God's image in man in the wider sense is meant that man is created by God the Spirit, the absolute personality is a spirit, he is a self conscious and self-determining finite personality. By God's image in the narrower sense we signify that man originally was ethically perfect, that is that he possessed true knowledge, righteousness and holiness (Col 3.10, Eph 4.24).

From these two determining factors, (i) God as a Spirit, immortal, invisible and (ii) man as a finite and ethically perfect spirit expressing himself through his body, we can ascertain the principles of true worship.

Worship must be spiritual. This follows from the spirituality of God. Any worship must be fixed upon God as Spirit. Never may he be thought of as represented by material or sensuous things. That would be leveling the Creator down to the level of the creature. This spirituality of worship is also implied in man's makeup. He too is first of all spiritual. True, his body is an essential part of his finite personality. From this it follows that man may and even must give external expression to the worship of his spirit. But this external expression does not reduce the spirituality of worship if only the external is used as a means to the internal. Worship becomes unspiritual or sensuous if (a) God is thought of sensuously and (b) if man used the external as an end instead of as a means.

Secondly, worship must be God-regulated. This is implied in the fact that God is the absolute Spirit, and man the finite personality. Normal worship cannot but be based upon revelation.

We do not here speak of the Bible. Original man breathed in God's revelation and will perfectly without any need of special revelation. It follows that if man cuts himself loose from this true revelation, he cannot know how to regulate his worship of God unless God once more comes to him in special revelation. After sin, it is imperative upon man to have his worship directed according to the instructions of special revelation in whatever form that may come. The story of Micaiah in the Old Testament furnishes us with an interesting illustration in this matter. Micaiah thought common sense was opposed to the regulation of Yahweh that all the Israelites should come to the central pace of worship at stated times. Accordingly he made his own little shrine and established his own priest, with the result that he came to grief for his disobedience. The principle involved ought to be stressed today when radio-preaching and automobiles once more seem to set sound common sense against the regulation of God that we are not to neglect the assembling of ourselves together. Of course, the matter of regulation of worship is not limited to the place of meeting but involves much more.

In the third place, worship must be mediate. As the first principle was derived, at least in part, from metaphysical considerations, i.e. from man's makeup as a creature, so this third principle is derived from ethical considerations, i.e. man's loss of the image of God in the narrower sense. When man was ethically perfect he could come immediately to God. With the loss of his image in the narrower sense, man cannot come to God except through a mediator. "No one can come to the Father except by me" (Jn. 14:6) In Christ does God restore His image to man. "And that ye put on the new man, which after God is created in righteousness and true holiness" (Eph 4:24). "And have put on the new man which is renewed in knowledge after the image of him that created him" (Col. 3:10). Now in as much as only in Christ is the image of God in the narrower sense restored to man, no one can truly worship God except through Christ. Even during the Old Testament dispensation this was true. Even then worship had to be mediated through the priesthood and the tabernacle which together prefigured the Christ. More directly still since the incarnation worship is first of all communion between the church, i.e. the body of Christ, and Christ himself as its head.

3.3   What is Forbidden

What is forbidden is naturally any form of transgression or neglect of any or all of the principles of true worship enumerated. And if any one of these principles is disregarded, all of them are. Any sensuous and sensual worship is directly a violation of the principle of spirituality in worship and is at the same time self-willed and immediate worship. Again, any form of self-willed worship is patently also immediate and tends to become sensuous. Finally any immediate worship is *ipso facto* self-willed and also tends to become sensuous.

It may further be observed that the principle of spirituality in worship was more grossly violated in earlier times than it is today. It was natural that man, once fallen away from God, should yet feel the need of a god, and that at the earlier stage of history he would seek to embody his idea of god in sensuous forms. He even made his god in the image of animals first because he dared not yet set himself up as god. Israel was in constant danger of yielding to this sinful tendency. Accordingly, when God was re-establishing the true worship of God in the world through Israel, it was necessary to give special warning against sensuous worship. In Deuteronomy 4:15ff God connects the idea of true worship with his own spirituality (Deut. 4:15). "Take ye therefore good heed unto yourselves for ye saw no manner of similitude on the day that the Lord spoke unto you in Horeb out of the midst of the fire. Lest you corrupt yourselves, and make you a graven image, the similitude of any figure, the likeness of male or female...."

The image made of God may first be used as a symbol to represent God in order to aid man to worship God. It is thus why the Roman church still wants to use them. Yet Scripture cannot tolerate such wisdom of man. God knows better than man in regard to the best way for man to worship Him. Besides, the image as symbol readily becomes the image as fetish so that God is identified with the image and the image is substituted for God. In this way a transgression of the second commandment leads readily to a transgression of the first commandment.

The modern form of transgression of the first principle of true worship often assumes the form of a hyper-spiritualism. Modernism's emphasis on "spiritual values" is a good indication of a lack of true spirituality. We may see this e.g. in Modernism's view of the sacraments. These sacraments have been so rarefied in their meaning as to be no more than vague symbols of a still more vague reality. The bodily resurrection of Christ is sacrificed to his "spiritual resurrection" and accordingly we are to seek "spiritual communion" with the "spirit of Christ." This strikes at the root of true worship since worship deals with the external expression of religion. Modernism is as unspiritual in its worship as was the lowest form of animal-worship.

The second principle of true worship, that it should be regulated by God, has been violated throughout the ages not so much through an expressed desire for self regulation as through a factual neglect of the true revelation of God. It goes without saying that the heathen nations do not consult the true revelation of God in order to establish the principles of worship. But the point not so obvious and yet true is that in many Christian churches very little attention is paid to the Scripture when principles or practices of worship are determined upon. Common sense instead of the Scriptures is the determiner. What seems useful from the point of view of popularity often carries more weight than what is actually taught in Scripture. In the recent argument about the woman's place in worship it was not so much a difference of Scripture-interpretation that prevailed as difference between those who would really consult Scripture as authoritative and those who would consider the needs of the twentieth century authoritative. According to the orthodox view, what the Scripture teaches will, after all, be best for the twentieth century no matter what the twentieth century itself may think of it for the present. Self-regulation spells the death of any church. Remember Micaiah.

The third principle of true worship, i.e. that of mediacy, is violated by all such movements that set aside or minimize the centrally objective redemptive position of Christ as the new and living way to God. Again we meet with various forms of transgression. We may note some of the more common.

In the first place, it goes again without saying that all nations beyond the pale of the true revelation of God in Christ seek to come into the presence of God, in so far as they actually seek to come into His presence, in ways independent of Christ. Sinful man can see no reason why he is not in himself good enough to present his offering to God. Sinful man resents the suggestion that he needs a mediator such as Christ seeks to be.

Nearer home come the various mystical currents of thought that have been in more or less contact with the church throughout the centuries.

Now there is a very sound and biblical form of mysticism. This mysticism attaches itself as closely as it can to the revelation of God in Christ and the Scripture and thereupon seeks to appropriate emotionally to the believer's joy and to the glory of God, as such as it can of the revelation of God. Alongside of, or as substitutes for this true mysticism, there has ever been a false mysticism that denies the need of mediate revelation and works independently of it. There may even be a hyper-spiritualism which denies the use or need of external expression of religion altogether underneath this mysticism. This false mysticism itself, when at all brought into contact with the revelation in Christ, consists of an attempt to elevate itself into a theory of faculties. It claims to have a private stairway to the great white throne.

In medieval times, Dionysius the Aereopagite and Meister Eckhart represent an extreme form of non-Biblical mysticism. In Meister Eckhart's case it was really no more than a special variety of pantheism. He obviated not only Christ as mediator but as well the distinction between Creator and creature.

Hugo of St. Victor and Bonaventura were less extreme. According to Bonaventura "from God all light descends; but this light is multiform in its mode of communication. The exterior light or tradition illumines the mechanical arts; the inferior light which is that of the senses gives rise in us to experimental ideas; the interior light which we call reason makes us know intelligible truths; the superior light comes from Grace and from the Holy Scriptures and it reveals to us the truths which sanctify."[5] Bonaventura thought that he could receive some individual revelations of truth from God. It is this that has made him and many other mystics unfaithful to the principle of mediacy in worship.

That the Roman church should be specially subject to such mystical deflections is due to the fact that it itself is weak on the very point of the centrality of the revelation of God in Christ. Its doctrine of tradition, papal infallibility, etc., have already broken in on the very principle of mediacy. Small wonder then that Rome has always been willing to harbor the most extreme mystics and how it has never set up any strong doctrinal opposition against false mysticism.

Among the Protestant communions there have also been manifestations of the same spirit. Of these we may mention various forms of Pietism

---

5.   Ozanan, *Dante and Ph. Th.*, p. 86, New York, 1898.

as well as the Quaker movement. The "inner light" idea is a violation of the principle of mediacy in worship.

More dangerous than these, however, more subversive of Protestantism, yea of Christianity are the modern forms of mysticism, e.g. that of Dean Inge, and that of Modernism in general, the imminent danger threatening Christianity from this source is concealed by the verbal homage this movement gives to the Christ as mediator. But its very doctrine that Jesus has taught the universal fatherhood of God proves that it has denied Him as mediator in any really specific sense. Christ, according to this view, has discovered the worth of the human soul per se. Accordingly, every soul can really in itself come into immediate contact with God. No one needs to go to Heaven or to Hades for us to discover what the way to God may be. "Look within" is the motto. Look deep enough and you will find God for indeed you are God. The Ideal within you is the reality of God. Thus says modernism. Thus also says modern pragmatism with its avowed hostility to Christianity. If religion can thrive without revelation[6] of any sort why then should worship have to be mediated through the Christ?

6.   Cf. Huxley, *Religion Without Revelation*.

The modern emphasis on the immanence of God which has virtually denied Christ's specific divinity and asserted His essential humanity all helps to develop this false pagan mysticism. Or one may turn this about and say that the false mysticism aids the false emphasis on the immanence of God.

Finally, we may note that much of the recent emphasis on art as essentially religious is due to, and a manifestation of, the same false modern mysticism. Often organ recitals are substituted for the preaching of the Lord. Or, less extreme, the artistic musical numbers are the really big features of a church service. Now, granted that art is essentially religious, and true art cannot be separated from religion—all art is certainly not in consonance with the Christian religion. As orthodox people we have no objection to the most artistic form of praising the Creator. In fact we believe that only a Christian can be truly artistic since he only can really bring art in connection with the source of beauty. But we are definitely persuaded that the Creator cannot really be praised except through the Christ. Hence art, if it is to be an element in the true worship of God, must establish its connection with Christ as the restorer of man to God.

Before passing on to the third commandment, we must still observe the threat and promise connected with the second commandment. The first thing to note is that these threats and promises really concern the whole law since the law is an organism and there is no good reason for limiting either threat or promise to the second commandment. Secondly, the threat and promise bring vividly to the foreground what was already involved, as we saw in the theistic background of the law, that God's own person is back of the law. Here is its final authority. It is the authority which man needs, without which he cannot live. Man breaks the law at his own risk. Breaking the law is a direct personal insult to the living God. We can never be separated from the judgment. In the third place, there is a difference between the threat and the promise in this respect that the punishment threatened in the law follows naturally upon the breaking of the law while the reward that is promised is a gracious addition. "So likewise ye shall have done all those things which are commanded you, say, we are unprofitable servants, we have done that which was our duty to do" (Lk. 17:10).

As to the content of the threat and promise we must first note that they are given to people that are within the covenant circle. Now, we have seen that the punishment once due to those that are Christ's has come down upon Christ Himself. The evil that comes to Christians is chastisement and no longer punishment. How then can God speak of punishment to Israel, i.e. the people of God? Because it is not all Israel which is of Israel. There are those that appear to be Israel and must be taken as belonging to Israel because of their profession, who yet in their hearts are not believers. Upon such end does such only punishment descend. It was not a later inserted idea of Ezekiel 18:20, "The soul that sinneth it shall die," which made men posit a righteous God, but it was a righteous God who said as early as Deut. 24:16, "The fathers shall not be put to death for the children, neither shall the children be put to death for the fathers; every man shall be put to death for his own sin" (Ezek. 18.20; Deut. 24.16). It is here that we deal with the ultimate issue of the matter. Yet this does not exclude the fact that in this life the children of God and the children of the world are often bound together in family ties. Equally true is it that God has laid down physical and moral laws that work in generations. God deals as a matter of fact throughout the history of redemption with individuals as members of the race. The children

of God are members of the redeemed humanity. Those not redeemed do not really belong to
humanity anymore.

Accordingly, it will occur many times that
children of believers may suffer the evil consequences of the sins of their unbelieving or also
of their believing parents. But in all such cases
the believer does not receive punishment but
chastisement and that not necessarily for sins
committed by him but that the glory of God
might be revealed.

4

THE THIRD
COMMANDMENT:
REVELATION

4.1   Remarks

FOR THE CORRECT understanding of the third
commandment, it is first of all necessary to understand what Scripture means in general with a
"name." We have come to think of names as con-
venient tags worn for purposes of identification.
But this is at best a subordinate use of a name.
In the "kingdom of heaven", each name is a significant expression of the essence of the various
members. We may even extend this idea. In Biblical theism, each member can have significance
because membership in a theistic system implies
relationship to God. On the other hand, in antitheistic "systems", no name can be more than
an identification mark since there is no system in

which there could be members. Even the identification mark is a theistic importation, since in a native antitheism there is nothing but unrelated plurality in which nobody can mean anything to anybody.

Now, since through redemption theism is restored, we expect to find that there will be some indication of the meaning of names. The "name" of Christ restores the center of unity. It re-connects man with God who is the center and fountain of all significant predication. Thus man is enabled to have a real name again.

Again, since in the Old Testament dispensation we have a more externalistic expression of the redemptive principle than in the New Testament, we expect that in the Old Testament, names will be changed more often as they are brought into relation with the covenant than will be the case in the New Testament. Especially those that occupy a place of strategic importance in the process of redemption will be given names that fit their station. Such names may be given at the time when the bearers are elevated to a higher station in the redeemed nation, as in the case of Jacob who is changed to Israel. Again the name may be given when for the first time some one is formally given a station of importance as when Abram and Sarai are changed to Abraham and Sarah. Again such a name may be given according to God's direction at birth or even before birth as was the case of the name that was above every name.

It is no wonder then that the "name" is of great significance. The apostles do miracles in the name of Jesus, and baptize men in the names of the triune God.

But if such is to be the case, the name of Jesus or the name of God must be more than "my idea about God." Accordingly, we find that in Scripture God tells his people what His name is and how He wants them to use it. The name Yahweh is not given to God by the people but by God to Himself.

The name of God represents His personality. It means something different for His people than for those that are not His people. The name John e.g. may mean much to his wife while for a stranger it means little or nothing. So God's people know the name Yahweh, because they are known, i.e. loved by Him. God has revealed His gracious purpose to His people in His name. Yahweh means the one who will be faithful to carry out His promises of redemption for His own. Thus when God in Christ has revealed Himself to you and you have received the full possession of this revelation, you express all this by calling him your covenant God, Yahweh.

It is no wonder then that the name of Yahweh becomes a bone of contention in a world of sin. Men will do for its honor or drag it through the mire. Even to be "neutral" is impossible and sinful, since it spells a high-hearted scorn of God's gracious condescending love whereby He revealed Himself to the sinner. There is not, because there cannot be, e.g. an impartial scholarship that will investigate the claims of the special revelation of God in Scripture which is no more nor less than the explication of the name Yahweh.

4.2   What is Commanded

4.2.1   *His People Must Know that Name or Revelation*

If the name Yahweh signifies the revelation of the gracious saving power of God to his people, then it follows that His people must seek to know the fullness of that revelation as far as they can fathom it. All men have some revelation of God within them, the voice of conscience, a yearning for something above them, a fear of their sins being found out. But the believer has had the cataract of darkness that is upon his eyes because of sin removed by the Holy Spirit. Accordingly, he can see the true character of the general and more particularly the special revelation that has come to him. Yet there is much progress to be made. For many of those that came into saving contact with Jesus while He was on earth, it took a long while before they fathomed more and more the depth of the gracious redemption they had received.

Private Scripture study is therefore a sacred obligation to every believer. The neglect of this results inevitably in spiritual poverty. Who can calculate to what extent the failure of private and family Scripture study is responsible for the fact that the church is overrun with Modernism? Modernism, as well as other *isms*, especially all manner of occultisms such as Buchmanism flourish when people are ignorant of the Scriptures.

The individual must have a systematic knowledge of the Scripture. Lack of it makes him the ready prey of Russelism, Mormanism, etc. Many of these sects claim to base their system on the Scripture and find no difficulty at all in quoting passages that sound as though they might bear the interpretation placed upon them. The Russelite will quote John and say that God is love so that there cannot be any eternal punishment. How will believers be kept from going astray into all manner of byways unless they can interpret Scripture with Scripture and thus have a full and rounded conception of the purposes and nature of God? Now the Catechisms aim to give just such a systematic knowledge of the Scripture. What better protection for the church against all manner of heresies than a faithful teaching of the children and the young people in the Catechisms of the church. Of course a consistent policy and the only safe policy of Christian instruction includes the provision of a Christian day-school and high school, in which alone a really systematic knowledge of the general as well as the special revelation of God can be given.

The collective responsibility of the people of God is as great as the individual responsibility in this matter of knowing God's revelation.

As "the body of Christ," the church must make provision for the training of ministers. The church as an institution is entrusted with the perpetuation of the special offices of the teaching and the ruling elders. Hence theological seminaries must be provided. It is not as though this is a common sense way of providing for the propagation of the truth only. It is this but it is more. It is sacred duty of the church to establish seminaries true to the revelation of God whether or not there will be any visible results. Those that are faithful may leave the future to God.

The curriculum of such seminaries will not be formed according to passing educational whims, but will be formed according to the requirements of the most effective way of teaching the Word. Naturally then, the original languages of the Scripture will form the first number on the program. Without a working knowledge of them one cannot really interpret the Scripture in the name of, and with the authority of Christ.

Then further, the instituted church is given the sacred trust of making known the revelation of God to the ends of the earth. Well-trained missionaries, such that can and will "rightly divide the word" are much needed today. It is not possible to calculate the sad results already with us because of the church's failure in this respect.

But the collective responsibility of the people of God is not exhausted when as the instituted church they have been faithful in teaching at home and abroad. As an organism, i.e. as a group of Christians not now conceived as the church, but in their wider relationships, the people of God must seek to have the name of God honored throughout the world in every department of human endeavor. The earth is the Lord's. Science, art and morality are the Lord's. Hence the obligation of Christian people to know and to make known the name of the Lord in these fields. To that end they will seek to establish truly Christian colleges and universities, fully equipped with the best technique in order to proclaim the name of the Lord over "the starry universe above and the moral law within." We may be quite certain that orthodox seminaries alone cannot stem the tide of unbelief. Their work is of a more special character and limited. To obtain a really effective Christian life and world-view, the average student needs more than a three year seminary course. It is not fair to expect our ministers to have a really comprehensive and really Christian view of things unless they are helped to relate all their interests to the one central conception of the name of God.

4.2.2   *We Must Confess the Name of Yahweh*

Confession, in the sense of making known the name of Yahweh, would be man's original prophetic task to perform. Man would be seeking the truth by implicating himself ever more deeply into the revelation of God. On this basis he would have realized what is now so often presented as being the real endeavor of science, i.e. the cooperative and mutually appreciative search for the truth.

Since the entrance of sin, however, war has come into the camp of truthseekers. They divide at the outset on the question where truth may be found. One group says that it cannot be found in God but must be found in the Universe as revealed in the mind of man. The other group says that this would make the search hopeless. Truth must be founded in God, and ever since the entrance of sin, in God through Christ. True science, too, must be mediate as we saw true worship has to be.

Now, it is the easiest thing for the Christian to tone down on his principle just at this point. Here, if anywhere, neutrality seems to be possible. Hence it is the sacred duty of the church to state the truth of the Scripture systematically in the form of confessions. It must bring these confessions up to date in the sense that as deeper insight into the revelation of God is given to the church in fulfillment of the promise of the Spirit, the church must give expression to this deeper insight.

There is a very pious-sounding slogan much in evidence these days. That slogan is "No Creeds but Christ." With this slogan, a self-deceived, well-meaning clergy seeks to gain new converts to Christ in a "scientific" age. What a poor service such a slogan does for Christ! Apart from the fact that everybody in reality has a creed of some sort, which reduces the slogan to the manifestation of a psychological absurdity, nothing could be less true to the spirit of Christ than to contrast Him with creed. He himself sought to give us a creed about God and Himself, namely that He and the Father with the Holy Spirit are the one absolute and triune God. The church has done no more than pass on the creed Christ gave us. A creed can, even in the nature of the case, according to the Christian way of thought, not be contrasted with the person of Christ. A creed is never anything more than a statement about the Christ. This statement may be either true or false so that true and false creeds may be contrasted but the statement itself cannot be contrasted with the person.

Instead of rendering a service to Christ, the slogan, "No Creed but Christ," plays in the hands of those who deny the Christ. It was the sin of Eve to say that there was no creed about God. The devil said there was not. He said God's creed about Himself was questionable. It was open to appeal. To whom? To his majesty, man himself. Did man by listening to the arch-deceiver get away from creed? No, he changed creeds. He now believed in himself instead of in God. For this reason Satan likes to question creeds about Christ. He loves the misty atmosphere of vagueness and generality. Cloaked as an angel of light he tells "pious" ministers that they must bring a person and not a cold intellectual principle. As though they were bringing the person of Christ if they neglect the creed of his divinity. If I am the man with a toothache I must know whether the man operating on my teeth is a dentist or a plumber. In such cases I do not shun the creed nor contrast it with a person. I connect it with the person that must save me. Thus the creed has the most direct and the most practical significance for me.

We see that the task of the church as an institute is to state and also to defend the creed. There is again the attitude of peace at any price. Ministers testify that they are orthodox themselves but do not move a finger when other ministers in the same church undermine the very belief in Christ as God. Now apart from the consideration that such an attitude would be considered subversive in any business organization, it is highly dishonoring to Christ. Those that deny the truths of Christianity are not tolerant. To call it a matter of difference what men believe is to deny the significance of belief itself. One cannot believe without an object in which to believe. Any carelessness about Christ's doctrines concerning himself or God is *ipso facto* a denial of Christ and God. To say that you believe in Christ as the son of God, and at the same time to say that those that do not believe in him are your brethren still in the Christian sense of the term is to contradict yourself. You do not in ordinary parlance say that you love your wife and children in that you have made no effort whatsoever to protect them from the murderer that slew them. You do not say that you are a true American soldier when while engaged in war you never moved so much as a finger to protect the stars and stripes. Failure to defend in time of war is betrayal to one's country. Now the Christian's task is a warfare. "Think not that I came to bring peace upon the earth ... " In as much as evil and sin are here, and in as much as Christ came forth with the avowed purpose to destroy the works of darkness, the Christian must fight, oft times for the honor of Christ (Tim. 2.10, 1 Cor. 11.19, Gal. 5.19–20, 2 Pt. 2.1).

The sacred duty of controversy is implied in the very task of witness-bearing entrusted to the Church's care. One cannot witness faithfully for Christ if one does not witness against those that oppose the Christ. If the knowledge of the name of Christ is to advance, it must advance in the face of obstacles. The "natural man" hates the things of God and will seek to oppose them. Only in the face of opposition can Christianity advance. It will meet with opposition everywhere. How can any faithful disciple of Christ, then, expect to witness for Christ anywhere without testifying against the opposition to the Christ?

In consonance with the preceding, we may observe that the preacher should make no mean apologies for presenting his message. He should rather speak with authority. He speaks not his own words but the words of Christ and the words of Christ may never be brought to men otherwise than with authority. The preacher does not sell stocks and bonds that may be redeemed above par at the bank of heaven some day. Nor is he advising people to take an interest in this thing along with other things. On the contrary, he brings the demands of God upon man. The judgment must always be the background, even when he uses for his text the words of Jesus, "Come unto me all ye that labor and are heavy laden and I will give you rest." Jesus offered rest but he also said that those who did not accept his rest would be cast out into outer darkness.

Applying still further the demands of Christ that we must confess His name before men, we may consider the matter of doctrinal discipline in the local congregation. It is becoming far too common in the church, this custom of sessions allowing any and everyone to the membership of the church whether they give reasonable assurance of agreeing with the standards of the church or not. Such a thing is unworthy of any human organization. To become a citizen of America presupposes at least some knowledge of the constitution of this country. Much more so then is it a sacred duty of those entrusted with the keys of the kingdom of heaven that they be reasonably assured that those seeking full membership in that kingdom know something about the love and constitution that governs its citizens. Failure to be faithful spells, moreover, disastrous consequences. Soon members admitted by no standard at all may be elected as elders of the church. What then can prevent the presentation of a pagan instead of a Christian gospel in the pulpit?

Finally, we may note that as was the case in knowing the revelation of God, so it is also the case in confessing the name of God; the duty of Christians is not fulfilled if, as the instituted church of Christ, they are faithful in all the matters enumerated. The people of God have in addition to this a duty to perform in wider fields than that covered by the instituted church. The world propagates the lie, instigated by the prince of lies, by the avenues of science and art. Accordingly, Christians cannot limit their propaganda for the truth to the word of the church.

Christians must need enter the field of science. If possible they are to train Christian physicists, biologists, etc. Such scientists are to investigate and interpret nature as the handiwork of God, never fearing the much lauded farce of "neutrality." So, also, Christians must enter the field of art to claim it for Christ. The damage done to the cause of Christ by non-Christian novels and literature in general is incalculable. A Christian daily newspaper may be an ideal impossible of realization at the present time, but it is a genuine ideal nevertheless.

4.3   What is Forbidden

What is forbidden is naturally a neglect of, or an open opposition to, the revelation of God. We might omit a full discussion of this point, by simply pointing out that a neglect of, and opposition to, the revelation of God will naturally reveal itself in a neglect of, and opposition to any attempt at knowing and confessing the name of Yahweh. We have already suggested several ways of transgression in order to make plain that which was commanded. Yet it may be of some service to enumerate some more specific forms of the general spirit of opposition to the revelation of God.

As the first of these we mention again the heathen nations. Their "search for the truth" is not as innocent a thing as it is often presented as being. Paganism is a deflection from an original theism or theism itself is not true. Paganism is antitheistic. If it seeks the truth, it seeks it in the Universe apart from God.

In the second place we may mention every movement in thought that appears in the midst of a "Christian" civilization and yet does not really figure with the revelation of God. Of course, all civilized thought has in a sense speculated on the phenomenon of Christianity. But the implication of the cross of Christ is that the very core of the human personality is corrupt. Hence, if Christianity is taken seriously at all, those that accept it must give "their thoughts captive to the obedience of Christ." Hence, a science or philosophy that seeks to interpret the nature of reality in entire independence of Scripture is *ipso facto* un-Christian. Not as though we would ask Einstein to go to the Bible directly. He deals obviously with the facts of nature. But when he concludes from the facts of nature that there can be no absolute God, he is not only un-Christian, but un-scientific. He has assumed the independent existence of the "facts" at the outset and therewith assumed the non-existence of God. Thereafter, it was unnecessary and impossible to prove anything about God. Thus we find that the so-called "neutral" approach in science or philosophy is in reality a negative approach as far as the revelation of God is concerned, and as such is condemned by the third commandment.

We come now to some more specific forms of the neglect of revelation. Of these we have several forms of occultism. Yet it is not always easy to distinguish the borderline between science and the occult. Thus in the case of telepathy, hypnotism and clairvoyance, there is not necessarily an avoidance of, or defiance of, the revelation of God. As long as they are operated by a keen human control over the powers of nature and for a worthy motive, they may be perfectly legitimate.

Spiritualism presents a phenomenon that is more difficult to explain. Even if we allow much for fraud, and more for a heightened control of the powers of nature, it remains difficult to exclude the powers of evil as a source of explanation. As Christians we believe in the actual existence of the devil. We believe moreover that he has great ingenuity. Our great comfort with respect to Satan is that he is entirely under God's control. Hence if we obey the revelation of God, we need fear no devil.

It should be observed that even if Satanic power is not actually operative through a particular medium, the medium herself claims to communicate with the "other world." Moreover, those that go to the medium expect to get through her a revelation of the other world. These considerations are sufficient in themselves for Christians to avoid Spiritualism. For the Christian, it should be an abomination to even attempt to go elsewhere than to God for the wisdom that he needs. If he goes elsewhere he has reduced God to the level of a magician. "To the law and to the testimony! If they speak not according to this word, surely there is no morning for them" (Is 8:20).

In Theosophy, a false antitheistic philosophy combines with occultism in order to lead God's people astray. In 1877, Henry Olcott and Madame Blavatsky published *The Isis Unveiled*. Now, Madame Blavatsky had traveled in Tibet where she had been in contact with the wise men of the East. This no doubt accounts for the atheistic pantheism of Theosophy. The pantheism of the Vedas is apparent in its doctrine of Brahma. Brahma is the eternal principle of all being. Now, the human soul is in its inmost depths identical with this Brahma, and is therefore divine. Similarly, theosophy's doctrine of God is that of an impersonal principle spoken of by the neutral pronoun 'it.' The world is a breath of this "it", and man, as a part of the world, goes the rounds with "it" in the way of rarefaction and condensation from and into the "it". It is no wonder that on such a basis no saving revelation of God is needed. It is not the existence of evil but the evil of existence that troubles the eastern mystic.

It is small wonder that these eastern cults are finding ready entrance into western lands. They find the soil prepared for them. Radhakrishman, in his book, *The Reign of Religion in Contemporary Philosophy*, points out that the idealistic philosophy is very similar to the eastern philosophies. Both maintain the self-sufficiency of man. Neither needs revelation. It is not so much an odd society of theosophy that the church need fear as the theosophical spirit of modernism within the church. The foe is within the gates.

The use of the lot presents a different problem again. The world cannot really speak of using the lot. A careless individual may make some important decision by fixing a certain sign. When he does this he is appealing to some fate or chance. When more scientific, he may use the law of averages as life-insurance companies do. Now, such use would be perfectly legitimate if it were recognized that they are no more than ways of God's providence, but when this is forgotten as it is when some computer tells us just how many human beings can possibly be born according to the law of chances, such use becomes antitheistic.

But what as to the Christian's use of the lot? It would seem that the first condition of any right use of the lot would be the recognition of the truth of Proverbs 16:33: "The lot is cast into the lap but the whole disposing thereof is of the Lord" (Prv 16:33). This is the recognition of God's providence. Now, such recognition at once puts God instead of chance at the back of the lot. Accordingly, it would seem also to diminish the occasion for the use of the lot. A genuine trust in God's providence is ordinarily sufficient to the Christian.

Then further, the Christian's life is to be guided more directly by God's special revelation.

This special revelation contains principles of guidance. It is these principles the Christian should seek to understand. Usually a clear understanding of these principles will save from many a perplexity. We are usually in doubt as to what to do, not because there is no guidance but because we have failed to observe it. If then in such a case we should seek for a personal dispensation of God's revelation, it would be dishonoring God, and we could expect no reply.

It should be noted further that as Christians we have the completed special revelation of God. Accordingly, we find that two forms of the use of the lot that were common in the Old Testament dispensation are not mentioned in the New Testament. The first is the lot of prediction (*Sors divinatoria*). The Urim and the Thummim were often, and legitimately, used to ascertain what the outcome of a course of action would be (Num. 27:21; Exod. 28:30). The second is the lot of consultation (*Sors consultatoria*, Josh. 7, the case of Achan or Lev. 16:8, the two goats). These two forms of using the lot, Christian moralists usually regard as belonging to the dispensation of shadows or as given for pedagogical reasons.

What remains then is the lot of division (*Sors divisoria*) used in the Old Testament in the division of Canaan. This form, if used upon the basis of the recognition of God's providence and after the principles of God's revelation have been prayerfully consulted and may be used by Christians according to most Christian moralists. It is then a most serious prayer for a testimony from God with respect to possible alternatives in order to settle a difference of judgment.

The oath is quite generally regarded as being the main form of transgression of the third commandment. The profanity of the street is, of course, a gross misuse of the nature of Yahweh. It reduces that name so full of holiness to an empty expletive. So also any light-hearted use of the name is dishonoring to God.

But the question now comes whether Christians may ever use the name of God in order thereby to testify to the truthfulness of their statements. Many have said this is unlawful *per se*. In order to ascertain whether this claim is Biblical we must first discuss just what is meant by the oath.

Now, the oath is the attempt of man to bring his statements into the immediate presence of God in order to test their truth. As long as there was no sin in the world there was no occasion to use the oath. Adam was constantly aware of the immediate presence of God. But on account of sin, man thinks of God as far away. It seems to the sinner that he deals with God on special occasions only. Hence if there is special need of truthfulness, man places himself right before the judgment of God admitting that God's threatened punishment may justly descend upon him if he has not spoken the truth.

Now, we find that God has Himself condescended to the needs of the sinner so far as to use the oath. This swearing of Yahweh made assurance doubly sure that God's promises should be fulfilled. "And said, By myself have I sworn saith the Lord, for because thou hast done this thing and hast not withheld thy son, thine only son..." (Gen 22:6). In Hebrews 6:17, a reference is made to this in order to tell us that Yahweh purposely used the oath to establish His covenant (Heb 6:17). The Apostle compares this act of God with similar acts of men (Ps. 95:11, Ps. 110:4).[7]

Accordingly, we are not surprised to find that Jesus Himself took the oath on that important occasion when He stood before the tribunal of Pilate. He did not use the form used today but He

---

7. Cf. further e.g. Ps. 95:11, "Unto whom I sware in my wrath that they should not enter into my rest." and Ps. 110:4, "The Lord hath sworn and will not repent: Thou art a priest forever ...."

used the form current at the time. The Apostles followed in this practice. "That which I write now, behold I witness before God, that I lie not" (Gal 1:20). We even find that God even commanded on occasion to use the oath. "Thou shalt fear the Lord thy God and serve him and shalt swear by his name" (Dt 6:1). "Then shall the oath of the Lord be between them both" (Ex 22:11).

But those that maintain that no Christian may at any time use the oath appeal directly to Christ's words in Matt. 5:36: "Swear not at all" (Mt 5:36). But these words could not very well mean an unlimited command unless we were ready to maintain that Christ Himself did not live up to this command when He swore before Pilate. Because of the Biblical data adduced, it will be necessary to investigate whether Jesus' words must need be taken in an unlimited sense. We find that they may and must be taken in a limited sense. Jesus opposed and forbade antitheistic swearing and no more. The Pharisees were afraid to use the name Yahweh in the genuinely theistic sense but they tried to find a realm of human things by which they could swear freely, without involving the name of God at all. As if all swearing by any creature of God were not also, though indirectly, a swearing by God Himself.

Hence Jesus tells them to swear not at all by any creatures when you think that such swearing does not involve God. Accordingly, the words of Jesus are not directed against those who swear with serious purpose appealing directly to God.

If then the legitimacy of the oath is established, we must ask about its use.

Who is to administer the oath? We have grown accustomed to the idea that the government has the right to administer the oath. Now, the reason that suggests itself at once for the government's high position is that it is in matters of government that the most solemn truth is required. Yet a further and deeper reason must be sought. The government has been instituted by God. Obedience to government is required of the Christian because the government is the servant of God. Of course, when the government itself is atheistic it reduces its privilege to a sacrilege and an absurdity.

Who can take the oath? In the nature of the case, a child or any irresponsible person cannot take an oath. But even a responsible Christian must be certain that he is truthful in purpose not only (*veritas in mente*) but also truthful in fact. Moreover, the matter about which he swears must be righteous (*justitia in objecto*). Now, when these three are present, (a) capacity, or *judicium in jurante*, (b) *veritas in mente*, and (c) *justitia in objecto*, the oath cannot miscarry. But we may still be mistaken in spite of the most careful precautions. In such cases we should cling to our oath unless such clinging to our oath would compromise the honor of God.

We come now to the related subject of Imprecation. In common speech the oath is not used exclusively for the testimony of truth but also as an expression of hatred upon enemies. Now, it goes without saying that such imprecation is antitheistic. Men often appeal to forces outside of God. If they really appealed to God they would also be very careful how they appealed to Him. The question now is whether it is ever permissible or a duty for a Christian to appeal to God for the destruction of one's enemy. We may say at once that it is not permissible unless it is a duty. If imprecation is wrong in every case the Christian cannot allow himself at any time the privilege of being non-Christian. To the true Christian it is no privilege to be non-Christian in any sense.

The modernist and the orthodox believer give opposite answers to the question whether imprecation may at any time be a duty for the Christian.

The modernist says no and the orthodox believer says yes.

The modernist appeals at once to Jesus' words that we must love our enemies and appeals even more to the "Christian consciousness," which forbids us to hate anyone. Thus he makes out his case quite easily it seems.

The orthodox believer is at once under suspicion of having no real love and no real Christian spirit in his heart if he maintains the possible duty of imprecation. His "consciousness" is *á la modernisme* not really Christian. But this at once brings up the question as to whose consciousness is really the "Christian consciousness," that of the modernist or that of the orthodox believer? Now, the modernist's "Christian consciousness" in no case hesitates to modify the Old Testament, nor even the words of Apostles, nor, if it finds it necessary, the words of Christ. Accordingly, it does not deem evil and sin to be so great that it requires a really authoritative power for its elimination. Experience is taken as the starting and testing point of all truth. But with this attitude, modernism has forfeited the name "Christian" since Christ and the Apostles plainly claim absolute authority. With this position modernism has also given up theism since theism implies God's absolute control over evil which control is gone if Christianity is not absolute.

As Christian believers we do not apologize for taking both the Old and the New Testaments as authoritative in the matter. Especially on this point, it is necessary to maintain the essential harmony of their teaching. There is a certain plausibility about the argument that the Old Testament countenanced imprecation while the New Testament definitely excludes it. The words of Jesus in the Sermon on the Mount seem by Him to be contrasted with the Old Testament. Yet this is not the case. Jesus nowhere contradicts the Spirit of the Old Testament. He only sets aside those that have misinterpreted the Old Testament. Jesus does, of course, allow for a difference of dispensations. He even maintains that God has temporarily toned down the absoluteness of His demands for the sake of the hardness of the hearts of the Old Testament believers. But all this does not affect in the least the unity of principle between the two testaments. Moreover, there may be a great difference in the form of manifestation on the part of the believer's experience. Due to the externalism of the earlier dispensation, God may require of His people that they shall kill the enemies of the Lord. Due to the greater internalism of the New Testament dispensation, God will not command such a thing. To kill an enemy of God, granted a Christian knew who was the real enemy of God, would be a sin in the present dispensation. But again, all this does not in the least affect the unity of principles between the two Testaments. Or what is the greater evil that can befall an enemy of God, to be slain bodily or to be cast into everlasting darkness of which Jesus speaks so much. Jesus tells us again and again that those that do not love God will be cut off from the land of everlasting life. Then He identifies Himself with God and says that those who do not desire Him as king have not loved God and shall therefore be separated from God. Now He expects that His own shall love God and Him with all their heart. And if they do they must have the same attitude toward the wicked that God and Christ have toward the wicked. Hence we find that only the most spiritual of the children of God, those most thoroughly filled with the love of God, have dared to imitate God and Christ fully by pronouncing hatred upon God's enemies. "Shall I not hate those that hate thee?" It is lack of true spirituality that cannot understand the imprecatory element in Scripture. The hyper-spirituality of modernism is a good instance of the spiritual flabbiness of the day. Modernism is so lovable that it would love the devil himself. Modernism has so much loved the devil as to put him out of existence. There cannot be, it thinks, anybody so evil; the "devil" is but a symbol of evil.

In the fact of this hyper-spiritualism, it is easy for Christians to tone down their demand for spirituality. "Then I said, I will not make mention of him, nor speak any more in his name." Such was the temptation of Jeremiah. "But his word was in mine heart as a burning fire shut up in my bones and I was weary with forbearing, and I could not stay" (Jer. 20:9). Such was the prophet's victory. Christ and His prophets and apostles are at one in saying that the kingdom of God cannot be established unless the enemy be destroyed. During the Old Testament dispensation, the Lord had separated His people externally so that His people knew directly who were the enemies of the Lord. Today this is not so definitely the case, but the principle that the judgment-day is a day of joy for the people of God remains unchanged.[8]

---

8. Story of Noah (Gn 5–25). Joshua vs. Achan (Jos 7.25, Ps 5.10, Ps 144.5–6, Ps 69, Ps 109); The woes of Christ. Paul vs. Slymas (Acts 13:10–11); "If any man love not the Lord Jesus Christ let him be anathema" (1 Cor 16:22).; "I would they were even cut off that trouble you" (Gal 5:12).

5

THE FOURTH
COMMANDMENT:
THE SABBATH

5.1   Remarks

THE FOURTH AND the fifth commandments
have a religious-ethical character and as such
form a transition between the first and the second tables of the law. The Sabbath and parental
obedience are of great significance for true religion and as well for true morality.

Secondly, we find that the fourth commandment is the only one that does not meet with at
least some spontaneous response in the sinner's
heart. We find very little trace of a seven-day week

among peoples outside the pale of special revelation. The Babylonians and the Assyrians did have a seven-day week but it is significant that the "*Sabatu*" of the Babylonians was considered a "*dies ater*," i.e. a black day. True, the day is called "*um nuh libbi*," i.e. a day of rest for the heart, but Delitzch had interpreted this as referring to the gods, i.e. it was a day in which the hearts of the gods had to be put at rest by means of sacrifice.

It is this circumstance that has led many interpreters to find in the Sabbath exclusively an ordinance of the theocracy and not an ordinance for mankind in general. It is therefore important to look into this matter of the origin of the Sabbath first of all. Even if we limit ourselves to the Christian Sunday, the question of origin is still important since it is then part of the larger question whether Christianity is introducing something entirely new or if it is restoring a creation ordinance.

Some have maintained that the Sabbath was first instituted in the desert of Sin (Exod. 16:22–30). But the whole story as here related presupposes a knowledge of the Sabbath. "How long refuse ye to keep my commandments and my laws?" (Exod. 28) This points to a formerly known ordinance. Secondly, the people seem to gather a double portion of the manna without being told. Thirdly, when some wish to search for manna on the Sabbath Moses is angry with them because he intimates that they should have known better. Thus the knowledge of the Sabbath is much earlier than the specific ordinances given for the Jewish Sabbath.

As in accordance with this, we may mention further (a) the fact noted above that the Babylonians already had a sabbath much earlier than the exile, (b) the positive evidence found in Exod. 20:8, "Remember," but especially in Exod. 20:11, "For in six days the Lord made heaven and earth." This last statement seems to point to Gen. 2:3, 4, "and on the seventh day God finished his work which he had made and he rested on the seventh day from all his work which he had made. And God blessed the seventh day and hallowed it, because that on it he rested from all his work which God had created and made" (Gn 2:3–4). In Exodus 31:17 it even says that God was "refreshed".

5.2   What is Commanded

5.2.1   The Creation Sabbath

If then the Sabbath is an ordinance of creation, this in itself sheds light upon the mode of sabbath observance. Man as a creature must imitate God his creator. That is a general rule and applies to the sabbath also. God himself did not cease to work altogether, [9] but from the specific work of creation. He turned to the enjoyment and the blessing of that which He had created.

If this had always been carefully observed two extremes might have been avoided. There is the extreme of legalism which over-estimates the external, making of it an end instead of a means. Against this legalistic extreme it is well to recall that man, because he consists of body as well as soul, is called upon to give external expression to his religion to be sure, but that the internal relation of man to God is always the most important. The temptation toward legalism has always been great since the sinner attaches false motives to his own deeds. He thinks all too easily that if he has only done what seems externally to be the right thing to do that the internal relationship is of less importance. On the other hand, there is the extreme of a hyper-spiritualism which depreciates the value of the external altogether. This hyper-spiritualism thinks it has Paul's authority on its side when it maintains that every day is alike and we need only hold the Sabbath in our hearts.

9. "My father worketh even until now" (Jn 5:17).

The temptation toward this hyper-spiritualism is greater now than it has ever been before since a higher but non-Christian civilization always exchanges the ethical quality of spirituality for the higher metaphysical status of the spirit over matter. Modernism has here as elsewhere adopted the pagan instead of the Christian principle and substituted a higher metaphysical status for an ethical contrast.

Originally, there was no reason for such extremes. The man of God was balanced. As a prophet he saw and emphasized the internal, as a priest he worked and emphasized the external and as a king he kept the two in balance. Since the entrance of sin men try to be either prophets or priests and therefore succeed in being neither.

5.2.2   *The Redemptive Sabbath*

We have now seen that to a correct understanding of the Sabbath we must see it first of all as a creation-ordinance. That is fundamental. Redemption seeks to restore creation. Hence no redemption ordinance can be rightly understood except it be related to its equivalent creation-ordinance. On the other hand, redemption is also supplementative to creation. Hence it is quite possible that there be a special emphasis on the

redemptive meaning of several ordinances giv-
en by God. Now, in the reasons given to Israel
why the Sabbath should be observed, mention is
made not only of imitating God's example (creation-ordinance) but also of Israel's release from
the bondage house of Egypt. "And thou shalt
remember that thou wast a servant in the land
of Egypt and Yahweh thy God brought thee out
thence by a mighty hand and by an outstretched
arm, therefore Yahweh thy God commanded
thee to keep the Sabbath-day" (Deut. 5:15). This
brings in the redemptive element in as much
as the release from Egypt is the first complete
typical expression of the whole redemptive process of man. As a consequence, true Sabbath
observance will always be colored by references
to the redemptive work as it centers in Christ.
Accordingly, only those that are in Christ, i.e.,
the believers of the Old and of the New dispensation, can really observe the creation-ordinance
of God. Here, as elsewhere, true Christianity is
theism come to its own. In order that man shall
truly imitate God, he must be in living contact
with God. Thus the sinner must reflectively turn
to Paradise past and proleptically to Paradise regained in order to see how the Sabbath should
be celebrated. And this the sinner can and will

do only if he is connected with Christ. Hence the Sabbath is also called a sign between Yahweh and His people. His people are to observe the Sabbath "for a perpetual covenant" (Ex 31:16).

5.2.3   The Jewish Sabbath

Having first studied the Sabbath as a creation-ordinance, and thereupon connecting it with the redemptive principle in general, we now turn to the various forms of Sabbath observance. That there should be stages in the form of sabbath observance we expect because there are stages in the form of the redemptive principle itself. Moreover, we also expect that since Christ Himself is the center of the whole redemptive process, that changes in the mode of Sabbath observance will take place in accordance with changes of Christ's revelation of Himself to His people.

As to the Jewish Sabbath, we accordingly expect that there will be strong emphasis upon the external observance of Sabbath ordinances. There were very many ordinances as to just how the Sabbath should be observed. Now, this emphasis upon the external is not as we have seen, opposed to the creation-ordinances as such, yet there is much more emphasis on the external in this early state of redemption than there was in the creation-ordinance. The reason for this is no doubt a pedagogical one. Redemption entered first at a time when the human race, in the presumption of youth, had rebelled from its Creator. It had therefore to be tamed with bit and bridle. The power of spiritual discernment, even when there in principle, was as small, and objective revelation adjusted itself accordingly.

In consonance with an emphasis on the external we find an equal emphasis on the negative. Parents more often say "don't" to children than to do because a child's perversity manifests itself directly in a destructive direction.

There was accordingly a very great danger to legalism in this early stage. Moses tells the children of Israel that they failed to see the end of the religious transactions in which they were engaged. That is, they did not comprehend that the blood of bulls and goats had not the least value in itself but only pointed to the blood of Calvary. Yet the people persisted to think that if they only lived up to the ordinances of the theocracy and in this case to the ordinances with respect to the Sabbath in an external sense all would be well. When this process continued and the people, instead of gaining deeper spiritual insight as time went on, fixed their eyes more and more on the external, that strange conglomeration of moral earnestness and spiritual equivocation that we call Pharisaism arose.

Finally, there is a point of specific importance to be noted with respect to the Jewish Sabbath. It is often presented as typical of the New Testament Sabbath only. Yet this is not the case. The period of the Old Testament is a subdivision of the whole of redemptive history. Accordingly, the common characteristics of the whole redemptive history come to expression here. Now, it is a common characteristic of the whole of the redemptive Sabbath, that it is reminiscent of the Sabbath of Paradise lost and also that it is prophetic of Paradise regained. We conclude then that the Jewish Sabbath foreshadows, even if indirectly, the eternal Sabbath that remains for all "the people of God." The difference between the Old and the New Testament Sabbath in this respect is that the Old Testament Sabbath foreshadows both the New Testament and the eternal Sabbath, while the New Testament Sabbath foreshadows only the eternal Sabbath. Moreover, the typical element, because more abundant and because appearing at an earlier stage of revelation, will be more externally expressed. And these principles we shall find to be of importance for the determination of the meaning of the New Testament Sabbath also.

5.2.4 Jesus and the Sabbath

We have already observed that since Christ is the center of the entire redemptive process the mode of sabbath-observance will naturally be determined by His deeds and by His words.

Since Christ assumed the true human nature, He also observed the Sabbath as a creation-ordinance. Moreover, since according to the flesh He was born of the Jewish nation, He observed the Jewish Sabbath. Yet He sought to restore and develop a spiritual understanding in the midst of the external Old Testament dispensation. Against the Pharisees, He therefore maintained that the Sabbath was for man and not man for the Sabbath.

Meanwhile, He carried about with Him the consciousness of His unique place with respect to the Sabbath as well as His unique place with respect to all the redemptive ordinances. His finished work, He knew, was to usher in a new era in the history of the redemption and therefore in the mode of Sabbath observance. Accordingly, He began to give glimpses of this, His unique place with respect to the Sabbath. Jesus did much healing on the Sabbath. Sometimes He seems needlessly to offend the Pharisees. It cannot be said that in the case of all Sabbath healings performed by Jesus that they could not have waited till the following day. It is not the priority of man to the Sabbath alone but the superiority of the Son of Man with respect to the Sabbath that must be brought in to explain such healings as could easily have waited a day. "The Son of Man is Lord also of the Sabbath" (Matt. 12:8; Mark 2:28; Luke 6:5).

Jesus, to be sure, gave no instructions for a change with respect to the day to be observed. But this is of little significance. Jesus gave no instructions about many things which He nevertheless meant for His followers to do. It is the fact of His finished work that is of importance. As to the instruction about the meaning of the facts that was to be given by the Holy Spirit promised by Christ to His church.

5.2.5 *The Christian Lord's Day*

With Christ's resurrection, He, and with Him His people, enter into the reality of the rest foreshadowed in the Old Testament. Not as though the fullness of degree of that rest is already ushered in. That will not be till after the judgment day. Hence the Christian Lord's Day remains typical still. But the typical is less externalistic, less futuristic, more internal. The reality is already with us since we are already "set in heavenly places."

The transition from the last to the first day of the week was accomplished gradually. Jesus apparently wished that His followers should, for the time being, still observe the Jewish Sabbath. "Pray that your flight be not in the winter or on the Sabbath" (Matt. 24:20). Yet we would today be acting contrary to the spirit of Christ if we should seek to reintroduce the Jewish Sabbath in point of time and in point of mode of observance. To do so would be to deny that by Christ's resurrection He has ushered in the true redemption from the labor of Sin.

The last day of the week was replaced by the first as the spiritual significance of the resurrection began more fully to be understood. The first day of the week was the resurrection day. A more spiritual understanding of Christ's work enabled the Apostles to see the significance of the resurrection. Jesus' own appearances on "the first day of the week" helped to fix attention on this day. The early believers began to meet on the first day of the week (Acts 20:7). In 1 Cor. 16:2, Paul enjoins the Christians to lay aside something every first day of the week (1 Cor. 16:2). Again, in Rev. 1:10, John says that he was in the Spirit on the Lord's Day (Rev. 1:10). Thelop. Brabourne is quoted as saying: "Woe to those preachers that try to prove from these texts." Now, we have no desire to prove the whole matter from these texts but only refer to them as corroborative of the significance of the resurrection. The real argument for the change of the day is the fact of the resurrection in its redemptive significance.

In further corroboration, we may point to Paul's argument against the Judaizers.[10] Some have tried to deduce from such places that Paul meant to have no distinction made between any days. That would be contrary to his general teaching and practice in which he has constantly set aside the first day of the week as "the Lord's Day." Moreover, the Apostle is definitely arguing against Judaizers. If the Judaizers got their way they would reintroduce the whole Old Testament scheme. Not to do this would not be an innocent out-of-dateness, a harmless obscurantism.

---

10. "Ye observe days and months and seasons and years" (Gal 4.9–11).; "Let no man therefore judge you in meat or in drink or in respect of a feast day, or a new moon or a sabbath day" (Col 2.16).

It would be impossible to reinstate Judaism. A Judaism reinstated would be paganism. It implied a denial of the redemptive significance of the very central facts of Christ's work. Thus sabbatism is not a harmless fancy. It is harmless in so far as inconsistent. If consistent, it would substitute the whole of Judaism for Christianity. Now, in the transition time, the consistency of this principle was not yet fully understood. Accordingly, we find that Paul does not militate against Sabbath.[11] Instead of Sunday observance, when it led to nothing further. Only when with Sabbath-observance the whole of Judaism sought re-entrance did he attack it hard.

Slowly through the ages the spiritual principle was understood. In Thomas Aquinas we have perhaps a high-water mark of development. The reformers in their zeal against the externalism of Rome often veered over to the other extreme. Among them the Anabaptists considered it unnecessary to observe the Sabbath in any special sense. In reaction to this, Bound published a treatise on the Sabbath in 1595 that ushered in the Puritan Sabbath with its great emphasis on external Sabbath-keeping. Thus, the history of Sabbath controversies once more established

---

11. He often preached on the sabbath-day.

the point that it is easy to fall into extremes. The danger of Anabaptism on the one hand, and the danger of Pharisaism on the other, have always beset the church. From these dangers we may be to a large extent kept free if we recognize in the first place that the Sabbath is an institution based upon a creation-ordinance. Accordingly, we are to be "followers of God" and like him "rest" from our labors. In the second place, internal Sabbath-keeping is of primary significance. We are to withdraw from all manner of labor and distraction that would prevent us from fixing our hearts in private or in public worship upon God and Christ. No amount of detailed external observance can ever replace this internal sabbath-keeping. Hence also, since God has made man "soul" and "body" and "soul" and "body" have their needs, it is well to note that a "Puritan" sabbath is not necessarily the best sabbath. We are to engage in spiritual exercises on the sabbath day but cannot engage in spiritual exercises unless we are physically fit. In the third place, the external sabbath keeping is not a matter of indifference. To engage in spiritual exercises presupposes an undisturbed atmosphere. If we disturb the sabbath atmosphere we sin against ourselves and perhaps against our neighbors. [12]

---

12. We shall not discuss separately what is forbidden in the fourth commandment since this has been touched upon constantly in the discussion of what is commanded.

6

THE FIFTH COMMANDMENT: AUTHORITY

6.1   Remarks

WE HAVE ALREADY spoken of promise and threat as related to the law when discussing the second commandment. The reason for noting it here is that Paul tells us in Ephesians 6:3 that this fifth commandment is "the first commandment with promise" (Eph 6:3). If this is not to conflict with the fact that promises and threats are attached to the second commandment we must conclude that in the fifth commandment the promise is attached to that particular commandment, while in the case of the second, the promised threat included the whole law.

As to the content of the promise we may remark that it cannot mean that every individual who honors his parents will live long. Nor did it mean this even during the Old Testament time. The facts would then have proved the promise untrue many times. It means that the nation whose citizens have respect for parents and old age in general may expect to endure.

6.2   What is Commanded

To understand what is commanded we must note at once that the fifth commandment is not limited to the family life but involves the general question of authority wherever it appears. The family is the unit from which society is built up, and for this reason it is mentioned and not society and state. But this does not allow us to conclude that the Scriptures furnish us with no basis for social ethics.

Even if we had no specific commandments with respect to social life, we would still have a basis for social ethics in the Scriptural doctrine of God. It is the theistic doctrine of God as set forth in the Bible that furnishes the foundation for all authority. We make bold to say that only upon this basis is there any authority among men anywhere. Without the theistic conception of God every law of nature and of morals has just happened to appear in a mere chance universe. There is then no reason why one human being would exercise any authority over another. The accident of favorable circumstance, greater strength, superior ability etc., are in themselves no justification for any human being to exercise authority over any other. On the other hand, given the Christian theistic conception of a God who is Himself the source of law and authority among men follows at once.

And even the nature of authority is then established. We speak often of moral authority. By it we mean that someone has by capacity and effort reached a position in society which causes others to look to his opinion as weighty. So a medical doctor has authority. But this is not what is properly meant by authority. By authority in the proper sense of the term is meant that one must, in the name of God require obedience of others to certain laws of God. Those that require obedience are God's servants. They have no authority in themselves. Nor is their authority directly delegated to them by other people. If it is delegated to them by other people it is because these other people are themselves the proper agents of God to delegate authority. In any case, all authority among men is delegated to men by God. Whenever any man fails to recognize this he usurps authority. If he is still obeyed by others it may be that these others look beyond him to God and obey him for God's sake only.

6.2.1   The Family

With the general theistic conception of authority as a background, we do not wonder that the Christian conception of the family is quite different from that of the non-Christian. We are not now discussing marriage. A discussion of marriage comes under the seventh commandment. Here we only speak of authority. But we must speak of authority in the family first and therefore of the family itself. If the family had originated gradually as man emerged from the non-moral stage of existence there could be no authority properly speaking. Or, granted there were a semblance of authority of parents over children, there were at least no reason at all to speak of the authority of man over wife. Modern feminism is right if antitheism is right. That man is stronger than woman, etc., is in itself no justification for authority. There is on the theistic basis no such thing as a law of nature apart from God. Paul speaks about nature teaching us certain things but he conceives of nature's laws as being expressive of the will of nature's God.

On the theistic basis, on the other hand, we must preface a discussion of parental authority with a discussion of the husband's authority. The law of nature teaches us the husband's authority. A family needs authority in order to fulfill its purpose. There must be unity and harmony and this harmony finds its final expression in the husband. The story of the creation of Eve is introduced by saying that she has to be a helpmate to man. It is with reference to this that Paul speaks in 1 Tim. 2:13, that Adam was first created.

There is nothing degrading for woman in this arrangement. That place which God has assigned to us is always the most honorable. Nor would there be any friction on the matter were it not for sin. It was as a punishment for her sin that God spoke the words to Eve that the natural relationship would become abnormal so that man's authority should actually turn out to be despotism (Gen. 3:16). It is in Christ that the true relationship is restored in principle.[13] "For the husband is the head of the wife, as Christ also is the head of the church ... " (Eph. 5:23) Paul indicates how

---

13. The sections of Ephesians 5 and 6, as well as Colossians 3, are important.

holy the matter of authority is. No one can afford to trifle with authority that is directly compared to the sacred authority of Christ over his church. On the other hand, no one can afford to abuse such authority since he really possesses it only as he exercises it in the spirit of Christ. If husbands love their wives as Christ loves his church their authority can never seem burdensome. If true love exists the husband will target the wife as "the weaker vessel," and consider her as a "fellow-believer" in order that the common prayers "be not hindered" (1 Pet. 3:1; Tim. 2:3–5).

These matters are not a cause for frivolity. Society is suffering seriously from neglect of the creation ordinances of God. Sin has wrought havoc in every phase of human existence. It is especially necessary in a case of this sort in which Christians are so easily led to follow counsels of expedience and plausible sounding theories of psychology, that we guide our conduct by the Word of God. Conduct so guided will in the long run be the more expedient.

As to parental authority, nature's teaching is even more plain than it is in the case of the husband's authority. The parent-child relationship is a natural and not a voluntary relationship. But even this would not in itself establish parental authority. If it were not that parents have authority delegated to them by God they would have none. Parents do not have merely a moral authority because they happen to be more advanced in age and knowledge but they have authority in the sense that they must require obedience. In the case of small children this may have to seem arbitrary. A child must obey because the parent says it must even if it cannot understand the reasons for certain actions. It is the parent's sacred task to cultivate in the hearts of their children respect for authority. Hence if they fail to demand obedience to themselves they break down at the outset what they must seek to build. As soon as possible the parent will have to point the child to the final source of authority; heteronomy must lead to theonomy lest it lead to autonomy. Indulgent fathers and mothers think they are but kind when in reality they undermine the family and society and offend almighty God.

In correspondence with the parents' demand the child must from his side obey. But Paul tells us that sometimes children may be "*a-storge*," i.e. without "natural affection." Add to this that parents seem ofttimes to be little more than brute beasts and what might seem at first to be a natural consequence becomes at once a moral question.

Only when parents really do their part can it be expected that children will do theirs. The children's part is to respect, obey and show gratitude. Even when parents seem ill-deserving, children are not relieved from obedience since the parents have their place assigned to them by God. Unless it be a case of obeying God's will rather than man's, children would be disobeying God if they disobeyed their parents.

It may be noted in passing that the best pedagogy of the day is beginning once more to recognize the value of the Biblical viewpoint in this matter. E. Hocking, in his "Human Nature and its Remaking", militates against the superficial theory of pedagogy so prevalent a few years ago that a child should not be taught anything with authority, least of all religion. Hocking realizes that unless a child is taught something positive which it is to accept as the truth, the will of the child will not really be developed. Instead of becoming a strong personality capable of responsible choice, the individual turns out to be a piece of flabbiness cast hither and thither with every wind of doctrine.

6.2.2   Social Authority

Coming now to the matter of authority in society we included in the term society all human relationships falling beyond the life of the family. But we may divide this in three subdivisions, (a) society proper, (b) the State, and (c) the Church. Now there are Christians who are ready to admit that there is such a thing as authority in the State and the Church but do not see that we need authority as well in the sphere of society. That we do need authority in society will readily be understood once it is realized that the whole of human life must be regulated by the laws of God. Wherever, then, true laws appear, i.e. laws that are really natural and therefore creations of God, they have authority for us.

Now, we may roughly picture to ourselves what the development of the human race would have been in case sin had not entered into the world. Family life would have expanded into group life. Thus the organization would have grown more and more complex. And in this complex organism, the unity of purpose required for the common task of subduing the world would demand an expanded exercise of authority. Thus authority in society would be a natural thing.

Specialization due to the greater complexity of society and due to differing adaptabilities would also have entered. Hence there would have been what we now call moral authority as well as authority proper.

But we can not now figure only with what society would have been. Sin has entered into the world and therefore also into social life. It is this that has brought in abuse and usurpation of authority into society in general. Despotism on the one hand and revolution on the other have been the order of the day. It was only due to God's covenant with the earth and its inhabitants, i.e. God's covenant of common grace, that prevented the total destruction of society from the earth. In Genesis 6 we are told that the imagination of men's hearts is only evil continually. Accordingly, God must destroy society. But for God to do so would be to defeat His own purpose. Hence we are told in Genesis 8 that though man's heart continued evil even after great punishments, God would no longer regard man's heart but His own covenant instead. He therefore put the bow in the cloud. His premise enabled God in spite of man's sin to continue the existence of society.

But as a means to society's continuance, God had to make an externally manifest revelation of His authority, for without authority man could not live for an instant and man's eye had become too darkened by sin to see the authority of nature. Accordingly, in society God sets apart certain defenders of His authority. The state is a gift of God's common grace. It has no authority of its own. Nor is authority as such vested in the "free people." No human being has any authority because man is a creature of God. But a creature of God can and must as a servant of God delegate God's authority in order that society may progress orderly. Accordingly, the primary business of the state is to prevent usurpation of authority by any individual or group over another individual or group.

Paternalism is the besetting sin of modern as well as ancient governments. A sad instance of attempted paternalism by popular vote was the recent efforts in Michigan and Oregon to rob the parents of their sacred right and duty to educate their children according to the dictates of their conscience. It is so easy for humanism in religion to reach for the weapon of paternalism in government in order to inflict worse than medieval persecution in the name of enlightenment and culture.

Abuse is easy. It is easy on the part of government. It is easier still on the part of those governed. The principle of authority requires that we be obedient to government because "there is no power but of God." "Therefore, he that resisteth the power, withstandeth the ordinance of God" (Rom. 13:2). And this is true even if the government itself is not fully conscious of this fact and may often have abused its power. Revolution may be a sacred duty but it has more often been a sacrilege. The French revolution proclaimed openly that it wanted neither Lord nor master. It may be noted that at such places and in such times as nations have most nearly adhered to the ordinances of God they have prospered best.

Still further, it was necessary for God, in order to accomplish His purpose with the human race, not only to keep it in existence by His covenant of common grace but to lead it to its goal by His covenant of special grace. A continued existence of a human race that has sinned against its Creator would have no sense unless this race has led on to its goal. And common grace was not sufficient to lead the race to its goal. It did not radically change the heart of man. Moreover, it was, in the nature of the case, a temporary measure pointing beyond itself for its full significance. Common grace finds the full justification of its existence in special grace. The world exists for the believers.

They are the salt and the light of the earth. Only those in Christ fully and really recognize

God's authority. Hence in the body of believers the true society appears once more even if it be in principle only. Christ is already king of the nations whether they are willing to recognize it or not. It is, therefore, the business of the church to maintain strictly the authority of Christ within its borders and to preach the true conception of authority for society in general.

We have now spoken of the State as an institution of God's common grace and the Church as an institution of God's special grace and have sought thus to relate them to, and give them a place within, a Biblical and theistic conception of human society in general. What remains now is society in the narrower sense of the term, i.e. society as distinguished from the church and the state. We have already seen that, also here, authority must need obtain since all law is of God. However, there is a difference in the way authority operates. In the state it operates necessarily by means of the sword. In the Church it operates through the Word. But in society it operates by nature. These distinctions are not absolute but at least are largely true. There is in society no compelling power given to definite individuals by which they may and must exercise authority over others. Nor does the operation of society as such fall immediately within the realm of special grace. But nature tells us that society grows more complicated as time advances. Accordingly, specialization of which the use of capital is but an instance, will necessarily result. Moreover, there are various capacities given to various individual men. Thus the ideas of socialism which seeks to level down all differences among men are contrary to nature and therefore nature's God. It is the abuse that capital often makes of its power against which a protest should be made and perhaps action taken. There is no doubt but that if capital and labor were both more theistic in their attitude, the friction between them would diminish. It is the cultivation of a genuinely theistic attitude in society that is the business, not only officially of the church, but also of Christian people as an organism. Really, Christian elements among all the strata of society should seek more intimate contact and as far as possible effect an organization.

We may note how the conception of society, state and Church as presented above differs radically from that of Plato and all other non-theistic writers. Antitheistic writers do not allow for special or even for common grace. For them sin is not something that has come into society by man's disobedience. Instead, sin is nothing more than an inherent evil unavoidably present in a developing race. Accordingly, the state and the church are thought of as no more than efforts on the part of the developing race to overcome some of its evil. And it follows from this that there is nowhere a realization that in every sphere authority comes from God. Right is right. It is a matter of getting away with things in a universe that happens to be what it is. It is no wonder that in such a case there is abuse of power and lack of obedience. It is only God's common grace that enables men in any sense to exercise authority aright and to give some measure of obedience. Christian people will therefore not hold themselves aloof from any and every movement in society or state that may in any way increase the legitimate exercise of authority and the truly theistic attitude of obedience. On the other hand, they will remain fearlessly "other-worldly" in the sense that they do not expect that genuine authority and obedience will be on earth till the kingdoms of this world are given unto Him whose right it is to rule.

7

THE SIXTH COMMANDMENT: HUMAN LIFE

IF WE DO NOT LIMIT the meaning of this commandment by a false literalism but seek to understand its spiritual significance we may say that which is commanded is to respect, preserve and develop human life. To kill, or as the original says, break up human life, is but the most extreme form of a policy the opposite of that which respects, preserves and develops human life. We may subdivide the discussion into that which deals with the respect, preservation and development of the individual, and that which deals with the respect, preservation and development of society, or rather that which speaks of ourselves and that which speaks of our neighbors.

131

7.1   What is Commanded for Self

The commandment refers to human life. It is not permissible to deal ruthlessly with the life of plants and especially animals. Yet the plants and animals are given for the use of man. Hence their life must be taken. Even vivisection need not always be wrong. If it be done in the interest of alleviating the suffering of man it may be desirable. But that in passing.

It is more important to note that the commandment has no limit as applied to human life. It is sometimes thought that we are at least the masters of our own life if not of others. But this exactly is not the case. We have no more right to do with our own life what we please than we have to do with the lives of others what we please. Human life belongs to God. He is its Creator. When one takes human life anywhere, one is stealing God's property.

What is more, one would be stealing God's most valuable property. God has created man in His own image. He has richly endorsed man with capacities for returning praise to God. Whatever the world has said with respect to the value of man is as nothing compared to the simple statement "created in God's image." It is impossible to clothe man with any higher dignity. Those that do not hold to the creation of this universe by God, have alternated in their charge against orthodox theology, between saying that it unwarrantably elevates man to a perch of privilege, or unduly lowers him to the position of a worthless sinner. It is, of course, small wonder that antitheistic thought should be so inconsistent. It always jumbles metaphysics and ethics. We are here speaking of metaphysics primarily.

Holding man to be created in God's image, theism has a higher conception of the inherent dignity of man than antitheism could have.

It is often admitted, even by those averse to the creation doctrine, that Christianity has introduced the idea of the inherent value of human personality. Now, in so far as it is true that Christianity stands for the value of personality as such, it has not introduced it but reintroduced it. Here, as elsewhere, Christianity has been restorative of an original theism. The creation doctrine is the very presupposition of the work of Christ. He came to restore to man the image of God in full (Col. 3:10, Eph. 4:24).

Meanwhile we should observe that even sin did not efface God's image in man entirely.[14] Man

---

14. See the Second Commandment.

remains, even as a sinner, God's image-bearer in the wider sense of the term. Hence it is this fact that man, wherever found, is the image-bearer of God that makes human life *per se* sacrosanct.

It is this fact that enables us to respect human life in general. It is this fact that enables us to respect ourselves. It is this fact that makes self-respect a human duty. We must respect ourselves because we are not of ourselves.

But the fact that the image of God in man is the only possible object of respect in him, involves the fact that only a Christian can really respect human life in general and only a Christian understands fully what it means to have self-respect. Christian self-respect is the only really human self-respect. Only a Christian really recognizes the image of God in man. He, moreover, rejoices in the fact that through Christ, that image of God has been restored to him in the narrower sense, i.e. that he once more has true knowledge, righteousness and holiness. Every Christian, even he of the lowest possible social standing, carries in his bosom the consciousness of being a true image-bearer of God.

Thus the natural instinct of self-preservation is moralized. Paul recognizes that "no man ever hated his own flesh," as something that is genuinely human. Yet, he at once adds, "but nourisheth and cherisheth it, even as Christ also the Church" (Eph. 5:29). Thus, even bodily life is brought into direct connection with the work of Christ. And this comports with the general teaching of Paul, that the body is the temple of the Holy Ghost. We find then that Christian self-respect is the only true human self-respect and that this self-respect is the recognition in ourselves of the image of God. We love ourselves for the sake of God.

A point of significance in this connection is to note that genuine self-respect cannot exist except a true humility be also present. And this true humility is not so much a recognition of the fact that man is a very small speck in a great universe. A crass materialism has advocated such a false humility. But a true theism recognizes the priority of the Spirit over matter. A true humility is the recognition of the fact that man has marred the image of God and that he is, therefore, ethically unworthy of God's love. It is this consideration that makes the prophet Isaiah say: "Cease ye from man, whose breath is in his nostrils: for wherein is he to be accounted of" (Is 2:22)? It is this that makes him speak the words of Yahweh: "I dwell in the high and holy place, with him also that is of a contrite and humble spirit, to revive the spirit of the humble, and to revive the heart of the contrite ones" (Isa. 57:15). Thus we see that for a truly Biblical conception of man we must keep in mind these factors: his original dignity as a creature of God, his ethical deflection from God, and his restoration to God in Christ.

When a Christian fully recognizes these elements, he is saved from the two extremes of self-glorification and self-abasement. Not as though true self-respect is a midway position between them. True self-respect, as we have seen, builds upon a theistic foundation. On the other hand, self-glorification and self-abasement are built upon an antitheistic foundation. When man does not recognize God as his Creator, he will quite naturally indulge in pride when circumstances are favorable or he will turn to a cosmical and individual pessimism if circumstances are unfavorable. The most extreme form of the one is self-deification and the most extreme form of the other is suicide. Of course, the utter folly of both is patent, even assuming the truth of non-theism. Man has certainly not brought himself or the universe into existence. He is derived from something else if not from God. Hence his self-deification can never be more than self-deception and by his suicide man can not take away what he has not produced. But at any rate, man does not feel responsible to God as an antitheist and therefore can freely make the attempt to remove his life. It is not a marvel, then, that there are so many suicides but it is a marvel that there are so few. The only way in which we can explain the fact that there are so few suicides is that God has by His common grace sufficiently checked the folly of sin in man as to make him feel something of his limitations and duties while on earth. Socrates said we have no right to seek escape from the post where the gods have placed us.

A caution should be inserted here with respect to the matter of suicide. We have said that a Christian will refrain from suicide. In saying this we have assumed, however, that the Christian knew what he was doing. But there may be moments of temporary insanity. Hence we cannot judge but leave the judgment to God. We are interested in the principle of the matter and this principle is clear enough. There are five recorded cases of suicide in the Old Testament. Abimelech took his life to prevent the shame of having been killed by a woman (Judg. 9:54). Saul and his armor-bearer committed suicide to escape being killed by the Philistines (1 Sam. 31:4).

Ahithophel did the same thing when his counsel was rejected (2 Sam. 17:23). Zimri burned the palace in which he lived and perished in it when Omri had captured the city of Thirza (1 Kgs. 16:18). Now, the Scriptures do not in so many words condemn these acts. They merely record them as facts as they do many deeds that are evil. Accordingly, the recorded suicides of Scripture do not affect its plain teaching that man belongs to God and therefore may not take his own life. The heathen saw vaguely that man is placed at a post of responsibility in this world. They felt it would be cowardice to seek to escape from it. Yet they did conceive of situations in which the *taedium vitae* would make suicide justifiable. Christianity can find no such situation. Life may be exceedingly wearisome for a Christian sometimes. But whatever is sent him, he is assured, is sent him by God and God will increase his grace with his burdens. The Christian will seek to be patient in tribulation. And this patience is not a mere stoic submission to irrevocable circumstances. The stoic good man and the Christian good man have in this respect nothing in common. The Christian is keenly and spiritually alert to the circumstances surrounding him. He does not cast about his shoulders a harness of insensibility when others scorn and revile him. He is rather a martyr for Christ, bearing all for Him, as Stephen praying even for forgiveness upon those that stoned him. "For whether we live, we live unto the Lord; or whether we die, we die unto the Lord; whether we live therefore, or die, we are the Lord's" (Rom. 14:8).

But suicide is the most extreme form of violation against one's real self-respect. There are many less extreme forms that we should avoid. Of these we may mention intemperate indulgence of appetites themselves legitimate, such as food and drink and sex. It should be emphasized that no gift of God is wrong in itself. Christianity has nothing in common with the Manichaean principle of the inherent evil of matter. Every gift of God may be used with thanksgiving. The Roman church has forgotten this with its celibacy of the clergy. Prohibition propagandists often forget this in their zeal against alcohol. It is the abuse or misuse of God's gifts that are sinful. No self-respecting Christian may allow himself to become a slave to any appetite.

On the contrary, every Christian should seek to preserve and develop his body and his soul. Any organism seeks to develop itself. So also the organism of soul and body should develop itself. The soul should do this by implication into God's interpretation of reality, i.e. by a true education. But, alas, sin has effected a separation between God and man. Hence man seeks his education apart from God. Consequently his "education" leads him constantly further away from God. Only a true, Christian education is really development of the finite personality. Only a Christian exercises himself in that which is genuinely true and beautiful and good. The term education is not a neutral term or a term always bearing the same connotation. Antitheistic education operates in a vacuum since it has cut the facts loose from God. Hence it does not really develop personality. Its apparent development is legitimate and advisable. On the other hand, bodily development is never an end in itself. The recent emphasis on physical culture and the craze about sport seems to forget that man is more than a body. His soul is often neglected in favor of the body.

7.2 What is Commanded for One's Neighbor

We may now turn to the social significance of the sixth commandment. And here it is our positive duty to respect, preserve and develop our neighbor's life and our negative task to oppose anything that would interfere with such a program. In short, we are to love our neighbors as ourselves. To do this is possible only on a theistic basis. Only a Christian respects, preserves and develops his own life for the sake of God. Consequently, only a Christian can really love his neighbor since his neighbor must also be loved for the sake of God. Non-Christians or non-theists have no center for their thought or their love that can bring man and man together. Each one is conceived of as existing for himself. Hence self-development is at the expense of one's neighbor instead of, like it is on theistic basis, to the benefit of one's neighbor. There can be no real community of interest among those not united to God through Christ. At most they cooperate for the sake of momentary utility. Dives was not really concerned for his five brethren on earth. He that had bound himself for no ties of love to God or man while on earth was not suddenly warmed with a love for his neighbors. In that doleful bliss the inhabitants have become like unto their leader, Satan. It is a warfare of every one against every one. If Adam thought, as Milton presents him as thinking, that at least he would enjoy the company of Eve when he ate of the forbidden fruit, he was badly mistaken. Due to God's common grace man has felt something of this.

B. Bosanquet tells us, in Christian-sounding terminology, that the individual must lose itself in order to find itself anew in God and the neighbor. Yet no true altruism can ever exist if God is no more than a correlative man. In that case he can no longer be the center and goal of thought and love. Disinterested love of our fellow man we can have, but have only if we have first loved God. 1 Corinthians 13 enumerates several of the characteristics of true love to one's neighbors. We cannot speak of them in detail. We may sum them up by saying that Paul visualizes his neighbor as created in God's image and therefore loves him for God's sake.

It is often said that what Christianity has contributed to the matter of altruism is that it has put away national barriers so that man was taught to recognize, respect, preserve and develop man whether he was barbarian or fellow patriot. This statement is only partially true. In the first place it cannot be sufficiently stressed that the altruism of Christianity is altogether different in quality from the altruism e.g. of stoicism. Christianity introduced something different than was known instead of only spreading more widely what was already practiced in limited spheres. In the second place, Christianity did not really introduce this genuine love of the neighbor but reintroduced it, because it reintroduced theism. And this explains the third place, why there were foreshadowings of a genuine altruism among Israel and nowhere else (Lev. 9:24).

From the preceding, it follows further that our love of God is prior to the love of our neighbors. Many today claim that the first table of the law has no significance for morality. One's belief in God is considered to be a hobby with no effect on one's attitude toward the neighbor. But the opposite is true. If God is what theism says He is, then we must love Him first and above all, and unless we do we cannot even love our neighbors. It is true that a lack of love to one's neighbors is a sign of a lack of true love to God, but it is equally true that a lack of true love to God is a certain guarantee of lack of true love to one's neighbor.

Still further, to love our neighbor as ourselves in no way conflicts with our duty to care for ourselves first of all. So also some neighbors, say, relatives, etc., are closer related to us than others. All this is due to God's providence. For to recognize this fact would be to contradict God's providence.

And this leads us to bring in a further distinction. All men are our neighbors. We must love all men as ourselves, i.e. for the sake of God. But all men are not Christians. And Christians are to love one another in a unique sense. Jesus loves his own with a unique love (Jn. 13:1). He gave them a new commandment that they should love one another (Jn. 13:34). It is the love of brethren that is constantly distinguished from the love of all men especially by John (1 Jn. 3:23). Modernism is greatly interested in wiping away this distinction since upon its naturalistic assumption it must teach the universal fatherhood of God and the universal brotherhood of man. The love of the brethren is that which endures eternally. On the other hand, the love for those not in Christ will terminate when their hatred of God appears in the judgment day.

Finally we must notice in this connection what it means that we must love our enemies. Who are our enemies? All that do not love the Lord Jesus Christ. They are our enemies because they are God's enemies. We saw that the holy duty of imprecation is based upon this fact. "Shall I not hate those that hate thee?" Yet while on this earth we are to love them as creatures, as image-bearers of God. In this world, the principle of ethical antithesis cannot and must not be carried out absolutely. Christ prayed for those that crucified

Him. But this should not make us think that Christ or His Apostles ever reduced the love to our neighbors to the prosaic level of Modernism when it maintains, by pointing to the incident of the woman caught in adultery, that there is too much good in the worst of us and too much evil in the best of us, for any of us to think that he is really better than others. Christ did not reduce hate and love to a colorless mixture of the two, but bade us keep them rigidly apart and yet direct them both to the same individual. And if it be said that here a miracle too great is required of us, the only answer is that all other possibilities are impossible. If love and hate were mixed to form a blend they would cancel one another and effect nothing at all; here is the utter powerlessness of Modernism. Its love includes the devil, and therefore means nothing when addressed to God.

If now this principle of true love toward our neighbor is carried out we shall have in thought, in word and in deed to seek to develop the general welfare of our neighbor. But this leads us to a further point. So far we have been discussing the individual's duty to himself and to his neighbor. Now we come to society's duty with respect to the individual. But has society a duty with respect to the protection of human life? On an antitheistic basis this cannot be maintained. On an antitheistic basis society is organized only for utility's sake.

It is easily understood how Nietzsche could deny society's right to suppress any ambition of the individual. Nietzsche had the courage of his conviction to ridicule Christian morality as a morality for slaves. But Nietzsche lived ahead of his time. His ideals will be realized in hell. God has graciously restrained the wrath of man sufficiently to give to society a certain sense of responsibility. Hence we have seen the state was organized on the basis of God's common grace.

And to the state God has delegated the power and duty to protect human life.

Human life is sacred. Whosoever sheds man's blood, his blood must be shed (Gen. 9:6). This is a sacred law for all time since it is based upon the foundation that man is made in God's image. The justice of God demands capital punishment. No amount of sentimentality can remove this divine command. Not even utility reasons or the consideration that time for repentance must be given. God will take care of all these matters as He sees fit, if only we obey His command. It is an indication that the "Christian consciousness" is not genuinely Christian, i.e. ready to test its standards by the standards of the Scripture, when in its arguments it does not ask what Scripture teaches but what Scripture ought to teach. It is a false humanitarianism that seeks to substitute the idea of improvement for that of punishment. Punishment must always remain the primary conception, since the justice of God has been outraged when human life is taken or God's laws have been broken in other ways.

Another manifestation of a false humanitarianism we find in much of the current Pacifism. War is to be sure one of the greatest of the evil results of sin. Shall we then say that since the human heart is sinful it is useless to put forth any effort to obtain universal peace? Such an attitude is to be sure to be very much nearer the truth than the superficial optimism that does not figure with sin. Yet such an attitude is not Biblical. As Christians we should put forth every effort to remove as much as possible by every legitimate means the consequences of sin. In this sense Christians should be pacifists in politics. But to say that every war is wrong and to refuse to serve in any war is false pacifism. The fact that nations, composed as they are of sinners, will often turn to policies of aggrandizement makes it necessary and just for those that are attacked to defend themselves.

But right here the final argument will appear on the basis of an appeal to the sermon on the mount. The contention is that Christians must never counter any attack upon them whether as individuals or as nations. The real Christian spirit is said never to oppose violence with violence not only, but never to require redress in any form. "But I say unto you, Resist not him that is evil: but whosoever smiteth thee on thy right cheek, turn to him the other also" (Matt. 5:39).

We shall have to examine then whether the words spoken by Jesus bear the interpretation given to them. In the first place, we must make the concession that Jesus' words must be taken literally. We cannot lightly and vaguely pass them over and think that Jesus could not have meant just what he said. Jesus expressly forbids His people to offer resistance. More than that, Jesus goes further and tells His disciples that instead of resisting violence they must offer opportunity and seemingly provocation for further violence. They are to turn "The other cheek." They are to offer the cloak when the mantle is taken, and go two miles when forced to go but one (Matt. 5:38–41). Even the Mennonites and Quakers have not always taught that Jesus teaches in this respect. They have often dared to go only halfway.

This interpretation accords with what we have seen to be the true meaning of love to those that are our enemies. Only the grace of God enables us not to turn evil for evil (Rom. 12:17), but to "overcome evil with good" (Rom. 12:21).

The purpose of this attitude we therefore see to be the winning of others to the same spirit. By heaping "coals of fire" upon their heads we are to make our enemies so thoroughly ashamed of their deed of violence and to have such genuine sorrow for it that they shall accept our position.

We notice now that a tremendous spiritual activity is involved in the attitude of non-resistance. Hence it is not at all similar to the passivity sometimes advocated in pagan literature. In fact, it is the polar opposite of the Buddhistic or Stoic principle so often compared with it. The antitheistic principle in whatever form it manifests itself presents a false imitation of the *ius talionis* principle of God. God is a God of righteousness. Accordingly, there must be punishment equivalent to the extent that God's law is broken by sinners. It was this principle that was falsified by the nations when each individual thought that he was himself the source of law. On that basis he sought to redress every violence done to him by wreaking vengeance on his adversary. Accordingly,

Lamech sang the "song of the sword," "For I have slain a man for wounding me, and a young man for bruising me: If Cain shall be avenged sevenfold, Truly Lamech seventy and sevenfold." So Habakkuk also speaks of the nations making their power their God. This was the logic of the position. But such an extreme method would soon have destroyed the earth. Accordingly, God by His common grace tamed the wrath of man so that the "wise men" began to see a certain proportion in moral matters and advocated an "eye for an eye," the so-called *ius talionis* current, especially in the empire of the Caesars.

But the universe could not thus continue to exist. A permanent redress to God must be made. The offense to the righteousness of God must be punished. Christ bore that punishment for all His own. Hence those in Christ must not and need not give place to wrath. Vengeance belongeth unto the Lord. All violence that is done is really done against the Lord. Christ identifies His disciples with Himself and Himself with God.

Yet this principle could not at once be brought into operation in its fullness in a world that had gone so far astray as the picture is given us in Romans 1. Hence God gradually introduced the principle. In Israel the true principle was restored. The *ius talionis* as current in Israel did not have the same meaning as the *ius talionis* current among the nations. It could not, since among Israel it presupposed theism while among the nations it presupposed antitheism. In Israel, accordingly, we have the true *ius talionis* and among the nations the False. Yet Israel's was no more than a prefiguration of the punishment to be suffered by Christ. Due to the general externalism of the Old Testament dispensation, the law had to be carried out externally by individuals or the government. In Christ, this externalism was done away. Hence the *ius talionis* has not been abrogated but fulfilled by Christ. And it is on the basis of this fulfilled *ius talionis* that those in Christ are to manifest their forgiveness to their enemies. They alone can afford to. But can they always in every circumstance afford to?

They cannot! They can as far as the consequences to themselves are concerned because even if they die they are the Lord's and will be received of Him. But they cannot if by their non-resistance they should defeat the very purpose for which they are to exercise the non-resistance. The very purpose of non-resistance is to realize the true *ius talionis* of God. That is, by our non-resistance we would have men accept "the righteousness of God" which is in Christ. But just as it was impossible due to the low state of the heathen to introduce this principle fully at once, so it is still impossible and will remain impossible to introduce this principle fully. The heart of man has not changed. Civilization has advanced greatly due to God's common grace. And this makes it possible for Christianity to appear without being at once annihilated. This also has enabled Christianity to develop some momentum. But even so, not every individual is up to the level of the general progress of civilization. And above all, if one is really to be won by the non-resistance of a Christian, he must himself become a Christian. And since he that stands upon the highest rung of the ladder of common grace has not yet set his foot upon the first rung of the ladder of saving grace, the policy of non-resistance may still be defeated when brought into operation upon the most cultured individual.

We conclude then that when the practice of non-resistance would more than likely defeat its own purpose it should not be applied. This is not toning down the words of Christ or His Apostles in the interest of supposed consequences. But in this case the action would be self contradictory since the very purpose of non-resistance is winning others. We have here an instance similar to that of the preaching of the gospel and testifying for Christ. To preach the Gospel is an unlimited and literal command but it is also said that we are not to cast pearls before swine lest turning they should rend us.

Christ's own example confirms this interpretation. He did not turn the other cheek when one of the officers of the Sanhedrin struck Jesus. "Jesus answered him, If I have spoken evil, bear witness of the evil: but if well why smitest thou me" (Jn. 18:23)? This example definitely proves that Jesus did not mean that His precept of non-resistance should always under every circumstance be applied. Paul followed a similar practice when he also protested against being unjustly beaten (Acts 23:3) and when he demanded that the officials of Philippi should lead Silas and him forth from the prison in which they had been unjustly retained. Now if we ask why Christ did not apply His own principle, the answer lies at hand. If Jesus had followed His principle, He would but have strengthened His opponents in their evil. They were too insensible to any justice to react in the intended way.

In the second place, in the instance of Christ's example and similar cases, society itself would be destroyed by the complete control of evil men if the principle of non-resistance were carried out. If then the purpose of non-resistance is to save society, non-resistance would be non-Christian in such cases.

Finally, the principle of non-resistance must be applied in consonance with that other principle already discussed, namely the principle of self-defense. We may not allow others to take our life. If we did, we would allow them to do injustice to God.

Surely, when this commandment is placed before the people of God in its rich significance, a great blessing for society may be expected in answer to prayer.

8

THE SEVENTH
COMMANDMENT:
PURITY

THE SIXTH COMMANDMENT corresponds to
the first commandment. The transgression of
the first commandment seeks to destroy God
as such and the transgression of the sixth commandment seeks to destroy man as such. The
ninth commandment corresponds to the third;
the latter defending the good name of our neighbor and the former the good name of God. The
seventh and the eighth correspond to the fourth,
the latter defending God in so far as He seeks
external worship, and the former defending my
neighbor in his external appearance. Of these
two commandments the seventh comes first,
since our bodies are closer to us than our possessions.

Besides the union of soul and body, which together form the mystery of human personality, God has brought individual human beings into union with one another in order to form a race. The human individual is not complete in himself. Accordingly, God created a helpmate for man and formed this helpmate as the complement to man both in soul and in body. With His own hand He brought the two together and ordained that from their union the race should be born. Only in the completed race could the image of God in man be truly expressed.

These simple creation-ordinances have far-reaching consequences. In them lies, first of all, the recognition of differences between man and woman. To seek to efface these differences is against nature. We find already in the Old Testament times that this was done. Hence the ordinances forbidding the exchange of clothes between the sexes, etc. Each of the sexes has a natural sphere of labor and the one to intrude upon the other's field of labor tends to wipe away distinctions created by God and usually results in sad consequences.

In the second place, the sacredness of marriage is involved in the creation-ordinance of God. God has placed in the race a natural attraction between the sexes. But this natural attraction involves also a moral relationship. There could be nothing moral originally; witness the absence of all sense of shame. Originally, the natural was good. We should be careful to distinguish this sense of the term "natural" from that often given to it. Often times the transgression of the seventh commandment is condoned on the ground that it is so "natural" to transgress. Now, it is true that the transgression of the seventh commandment is particularly "natural" since the entrance of sin, but this is because sin has made the true natural to be "natural" in the sense of sinful.

Accordingly, we also find in the third place that in order to obtain a truly Biblical idea of the relation of the sexes, one must not begin by admitting something of this unnatural "natural" to be genuinely and originally natural. Rome makes its mistake here. Its entire asceticism, and in particular its celibacy of the clergy, is based upon the supposition that the original natural is evil to a certain extent. Hence they who are to be most spiritual must abstain from contact with the natural as far as possible. Thus Rome's position is not merely a return to the Old Testament dispensation, when there were peculiar ordinances with respect to marriage etc. for the priesthood. On the contrary,

Rome's position is rather a reintroduction of semi-paganism. The Old Testament ordinances were not given on the assumption of the inherent evil of matter but upon the assumption that man had spoiled the natural. Even the Roman Catholic elevation of marriage to the position of a sacrament does not escape the charge of being born of a semi-pagan principle. Sacraments in the Christian church have to do with redemption and not with creation-ordinances. And though it is true and important that redemption has restored the true significance of the natural, and therefore has restored the sacredness of marriage too; this sacredness does not involve but rather excludes the sacrament. It is exactly because Rome has not clearly insisted on the original sacredness of marriage that it has afterward been driven to make of marriage a sacrament.

Then further, the sacredness of childhood is involved in the creation ordinance. It would seem to be more than unbridled fancy or unjustifiable allegory to see in the family, consisting of father, mother and child, an analogy of the trinity. The human race, not merely the human individual, is to express analogically something of the mystery of the godhead. And one of the greatest mysteries of the godhead is the eternal interaction of the three persons of the godhead. Hence, only in the trinity of the family could something of this be expressed. Hence, also, any interference with the process of the human family for trivial reasons is an interference with the plan of God. It would seem to be safe to say that the birth-control literature of the day is almost always motivated by the antitheistic conception that human life belongs to man instead of to God.

Still further, the originality of monogamous marriage is implied in the creation-ordinance. This is not only the case because God brought Eve to Adam as it were with His own hand. This is significant. Equally direct is the word of Christ that the concessions made with respect to the Old Testament times do not in the least modify the original monogamous ordinances. But the very fact that God directly created only one man and one woman lies back of these words of Jesus, moreover, we have seen that only by monogamous marriage could the family rise that should really be expressive of the trinity of God. Thus we see that monogamous marriage precedes special revelation. Redemption restored also this, but did not for the first time introduce it.

How radically the current evolutionary conception of the origin and nature of marriage and the family is opposed to our position cannot readily be observed. It should be observed that the current view is not based upon the discovery of facts by modern anthropology. Does anthropology prove that the sexual relationship was originally promiscuous? Does anthropology teach that marriage and the family have gradually arisen to what we now see them to be from the non-moral sphere of life below? We deny that it has. We deny that it can. The climate of the whole matter cannot even be touched by any historical science. The crux of the matter must be fought out between theism and antitheism as two deadly opposed systems of philosophy. As far as the facts are concerned, they do not militate against an original monogamous marriage instituted by God.

Sin has wrought havoc with every ordinance of God and has wrought the greatest possible havoc here. The first chapter of Romans gives us some idea of the havoc made. Every normal relation has been subverted. Even in the name of religion, the grossest immoralities were perpetrated. And Paul tells us that he dare not even speak of the full length to which matters have gone. The church fathers consequently often spoke as though the very nature of sin could be expressed in the word *concupiscence*.

Antitheism can, in all this, see no cause for moral disapprobation. For it, "what is", is right. At most it can speak of the disfiguring detritus of the seaweeds of the deep when it sees humanity but slowly emerging from animal practice. Accordingly, the utmost sagacity is expended to find excuse for that which is a downright transgression of God's law. Or what else is companionate marriage? And what else is the Bolshevistic conception of marriage but the logical conclusion of the antitheistic motif in this matter? It is only due to a measure of God's common grace that has restrained the full fruition of this antitheistic principle. Due to common grace, in connection with the by-products of Christianity, civilization has been able to some extent to enchain the evil beast of sin. But we are told that, in the future, the measure of common grace will be reduced so that chaos will develop to the extent that men will even lose their natural affection.

It is only with this background that we can understand the Christian marriage and the Christian family. Christianity is here as elsewhere restorative. And this is true of the Old Testament dispensation as well as of the New. The only difference is that during the New Dispensation the restorative principle can and must be more thoroughly realized. We have already seen that Christ himself said that the lower Old Testament position was a matter of toleration due to circumstances.

The heart of the redemptive idea of marriage is that it symbolizes the relation of the Church to Christ its head. And since Christ restores man to God, marriage symbolizes the entire covenant relationship between God and His people. It is this that makes marriage, if possible, even more beautiful and sacred than it already was as a creation-ordinance.

Only thus do we understand why the idea of marriage is given such prominence in connection with the covenant-idea during the Old Testament. Israel, as the people of God, is presented as the bride of Yahweh. The entire prophecy of Hosea plays upon this one motif. Yahweh expects His bride to be spotlessly pure. Idolatry is fornication. And the great love of Yahweh is expressed in His willingness to receive again into His bosom His terribly unfaithful spouse. She was unworthy of His choice in the first place. And having been made His choice she makes herself untrustworthy again and again. Yet Yahweh loves her and cleanses her of all impurity.

In the New Testament the same idea is carried forth. As an aspect of this idea, we may note Paul's emphasis upon the body as a temple of the holy Ghost (1 Cor. 6:19; 2 Cor. 6:16). Through His Holy Spirit, Christ is bringing His own, His bride, into close relationship with Himself. If this is to be fully accomplished, the whole personality, body as well as soul, must belong to Christ. Hence the Holy Ghost dwells even in the bodies of those that are Christ's. The Christian is "not his own" but Christ's. Bodily impurity is therefore a direct insult to Christ and His redeeming love. Those that are "bought with a price" have entrusted to their care Christ's treasures. Yet the temptation is so great just at this point. Hence Paul's emphasis upon purity. That purity must be internal first of all. A Christian must especially control his thoughts and imagination. Accordingly, he should avoid that which is suggestive of evil. Does the movie which sometimes advertises itself as "erotic, erratic, exotic, fantastic, fatalistic and futuristic," help the Christian young boy or girl to be pure in his or her imagination? And lack of internal purity leads to external impurity in word or in deed which is so expressly forbidden in the New Testament. Impurity makes a Christian unfit for work that is of value for the kingdom of Christ. It retards or prevents a free prayer-life and therefore true spirituality for the individual and easily becomes a cause for reviling on the part of the world.

More centrally, however, does the fact that marriage symbolizes the relation of Christ to His own appear when we consider the church as a whole instead of its individual members. We have already seen that it was the people as a whole that figured as the bride of the covenant God in the Old Testament. This same idea comes to its final climax in the book of Revelation. The world is presented as the great harlot, and the church is the bride. And the future life in glory is presented as the uninterrupted and unalloyed union of Christ the bridegroom and the Church, His bride.

How holy then and how beautiful is love, twice glorified withal. He that sins against it sins against his own life, his Creator and his Redeemer.

To inculcate this Christian theistic conception of love and of marriage is the privilege of Christian ministers and Christian people. If then, sin has been and is so exceptionally virulent in this sphere, it would seem to be altogether in order to sound a special note of warning against any influence within or beyond the home that would make it more difficult to live up to the demands of Christ. The enemy within the gate is too dangerous for Christians to trifle with enemies beyond the gate. One thing in particular may be mentioned: How can any Christian hope to express anything of the beautiful relationship of Christ to the church if he marries one that is an unbeliever? Fixed marriages are very easily consummated in times when the lines between the Church and the world are very dim. Worldliness allowed at one place leads to worldliness in other places. Hence the sacred duty of Christian parents to provide the most wholesome atmosphere within and beyond the home, the cleanest and best of amusement and association. It is more difficult than it used to be for a young man to keep his way. Only if in every respect he is taught to keep it according to the word will he escape pitfalls and snares and at the same time express something in this life of that love of Christ which He has for His own.

9

THE EIGHTH COMMANDMENT: PROPERTY

THE MEANING OF THIS commandment can be summed up by saying that it asks of man to respect, preserve and develop his own and his neighbor's property. But this presupposes man's right to have property. Accordingly, it is this presupposition that must be tested first. Now, in order to do this we must go back to creation first of all. Whatever is logically deducible with respect to man and his sphere of activity from the fact that he is a creature can be said to be well founded in Scripture as anything could be. Now, since man is created soul and body, he needs an external sphere in which he can act freely. He needs this sphere in connection and conjointly with others since together they form unity, but he also needs a sphere for himself where he can develop himself in relative independence. Property gives freedom for rational and moral activity.

Sin made man deny that he was a creature subject to God's laws. Accordingly, he looked upon this world as just being there somehow. Thus it was up to every man to grasp of it what he could. Moreover, when one had succeeded in grasping a portion of it, he felt he could do with it whatsoever he pleased without responsibility to fellowman or to God. The result was that if anyone was by reason of strength successful in drawing to himself much land, he would develop a theory of property-right which was a counterfeit of the theistic one. He has said it was necessary for society. This is true, but not the final basis of property-right, since there is no reason why society should exist unless it be for God. It was no wonder then that aggrandizement knew no bounds. When money was invented to become representative of, or even a substitute for property, the spirit of aggrandizement increased. Especially when, due to the increase of commerce and trade, money could be made to increase itself by mere investment, it enabled men to act as veritable gods upon the earth. Those less fortunate than themselves were despised and reduced to pieces of property. Slavery was the natural result of the abuse of the original legitimate right to property. In slavery, the thing has really reached its climax. Thus two extremes developed. The extremely rich lost all sense of responsibility and the extremely poor lost all sense of self-respect. To consider one's self the property of God is ennobling; to know one's self a slave of the selfish sinner is degrading.

Thus class-wars arose and were relatively justified. If neither party recognized God as Creator, it is the logical procedure, and altogether legitimate, to organize and use force to make elbow room for one's self. The world is then a free-for-all.

"Might is right." It was on this principle that the wealthy property owners, manufacturers and financiers have often worked. Hypocritically, or under an illusion that they defended their position with pious language. More straight forward and more logical, Karl Marx wrote his, "*Das Kapital*." In it he frankly embraced a materialistic and therefore necessitarian philosophy of history. The evolution hypothesis has further strengthened his ideas. Man, and therefore morality and rationality, have derived from the non-moral and irrational. Only utility can restrain men from seeking to grasp everything. Governments, themselves derived from such a society, have no higher power than that derived from society. Hence such governments too can only advise two wolves that it would be disadvantageous to devour one another.

The reason why all this has not accomplished the destruction of society is due to God's common grace. By it, he has restrained men's sin. Only now and then a Lamech, or a Nietzsche appears. To most men, and especially to men in high authority, God has graciously given some sense of honesty and responsibility. He has even caused these blessings of common grace to develop through the ages, so that more orderly governments and societies have developed. Yet, as time goes on, and men have fully demonstrated their unworthiness even of these temporal blessings, the days of Noah shall return, and we shall hear of wars and rumors of wars. When men have lost their "natural affection", they will be adulterers and robbers and liars. The irony of hell will be that men shall seek to exercise to the full all these "gifts" of theirs but find no field for their exercise.

Into this world of sin came the redemptive principle issuing from Christ its center. It restored in principle the true idea of property. We see this already in the Old Testament, and more fully in the New. The first point that needed restoration was the very idea of creation. Once this is done, the abuses of the rich and dissatisfaction of the poor will naturally disappear. "And the land shall not be sold in perpetuity; for the land is mine: for ye are strangers and sojourners with me" (Lv 25:23). If the land is the Lord's, and consequently, everything useful for man is the Lord's, man can be no more than a steward who will certainly have to give an account of his stewardship. Certainly, in that case, one man cannot reduce his equal to a piece of property. His fellow man has a right to property with him.

During the Old Testament, this principle could not yet be brought into effect fully.

Hence the Jews were not yet directly forbidden to reduce foreigners to slavery. Only in the New Testament times could this principle be more fully expressed. Similarly, during the Old Testament dispensation, the excesses of wealth and poverty were checked by the regulation that every seven years property should revert to its original owners or their heirs.

In Jesus' time, as well as otherwise, the Jews had sadly abused these theocratic-theistic ordinances of God. The Pharisees had added so many burdens to the ones prescribed in the Old Testament that the poor man could never expect to bear them. Accordingly, the greater part of the poor were heartless and discouraged. What in the midst of all this does Jesus do?

He does what we would expect Him to do as the restorer of theism. He does not necessarily express Himself fully on the matter. He did not do this with respect to the Sabbath. In both cases, He left much to be worked out later by His followers. Yet the principles are clear.

Jesus' utterances that have a direct bearing upon the question corroborate our expectation that He will seek to restore a true theism. "No one can serve two masters; for either he will hate the one, and love the other; or else he will hold to one, and despise the other. Ye cannot serve God and mammon" (Matt. 6:24). "And I say unto you, Make to yourselves friends by means of the mammon of unrighteousness; that, when it shall fail, they may receive you into eternal tabernacles" (Lk. 16:9). "If therefore ye have not been faithful in the unrighteous mammon, who will commit to your trust the true riches" (Lk. 16:11). "Ye cannot serve God and Mammon" (Mk. 6:24). By the term Mammon, anything of earthly value, i.e. property in general and money in particular, is meant. Jesus recognizes first of all that it is legitimate and necessary to have money. If this were not so, He could not have recommended its use as a means by which to acquire friends. He simply takes the creation-ordinance for granted, as it had been re-expressed in the Old Testament words, "the land is mine." Secondly, Jesus recognizes the abuse made of that which in itself is legitimate. When men had denied that God was the owner of money, then money had become their God. Against such, Jesus says that they cannot serve two masters. His own practice was in accordance with His expressed principle. There is no evidence that Jesus and His disciples were very poor. They had a purse and sometimes relieved the poor. Nor was He a dreamer with no eye for the social need. He helped the wealthy centurion and the poor sick man of Bethesda, wealthy Jairus and poor Bartimeus. Dives does not "lift up his eyes in torment" because he was wealthy, but because he had despised Moses and the Prophets who told him to make proper use of his riches. Jesus did, however, in this parable and also in his recommendation to the rich young ruler, indicate that riches are a great temptation, to which one possessing riches will easily yield to the loss of his own soul. Whatever may have been the specific reason for Jesus' requirement that the young ruler sell all he had, so much is clear that Jesus considered it necessary for this particular man to dispose of his wealth in order to be a disciple of Jesus. The refusal of the young ruler shows not only that he was not ready to give all for Jesus, but that he was not ready to give any to Jesus. He looked upon his wealth as absolutely and not derivatively his own. Riches are not wrong in themselves, but easily become wrong for sinful man.

We see then that the important thing for Christians to observe with respect to the matter of possessions is that private property is to be respected, protected and developed. Every legitimate means by which this is made more easily possible should receive our encouragement and aid. The total unnatural living conditions in modern cities tend, as we saw, to facilitate the breaking of all commandments and especially the commandments that pertain directly to social life. Individual theft and gangsterism are afforded a wonderful opportunity for operation in large cities. In so far as centralization of manufacture and industry is unavoidable, measures must be taken that shall make such centralization possible and consistent with the protection of life and property. Hence the preacher of the gospel will not preach "the social gospel" only, but will certainly proclaim to men the message of Christianity with respect to social life. That message is that men must be theists. If they are, the problem of capital and labor, of socialism and communism will not be solved completely offhand, but they will be solved in principle. A theistic capitalist cannot reduce his fellowman to a piece of property. A theistic laborer will recognize created differences among men and will be satisfied with his daily bread. Of course, as long as sin will last, the consequences of sin will last. Hard labor will be necessary, and men will seek to escape it by transferring it to others. Hence it may be necessary for others to organize and protest. And especially since we know right well that not all men have faith, it will not only be necessary for those that have to say to those that have not that they also have faith, but it will also be necessary to utilize every legitimate effort to make life, such as it is, as tolerable as possible. The Christian should help to remove the injustice of man to man. Since the entrance of sin man has been man's wolf.

Alas for poor modernism! It has thought to bring the message of Jesus closer to men when it gave up speculation about such "abstract" doctrines as that of creation. It has rewritten "theology as an empirical science." It seeks really to help social needs with "the social gospel." But its denial of theism of which creation is the directly significant point in this connection has made it impossible for modernism to offer anything to the struggle between capital and labor than that which capital and labor already know too well, namely that "might makes right." Modernism has wisely limited itself largely to the external, for truly, the internal it cannot touch. It can salve the surface, but not operate for major internal diseases.

Only orthodox Christianity has a real message for those engaged in "the struggle for existence."

The final message that it brings is the promise of the future. Modernism has emphasized the fact that we must help men for this life rather than comfort them with the prospect of the next. The sad result has been that modernism has had no message at all, either for this life or for the next. He that has no message for the next life can have no message for this life. If there is no next life there is no message from anybody to anybody about anything. Idealists of every age have felt the need of a "Beyond." Plato's "Ideas," Kant's "Noumenon," and Hegel's "Absolute" are evidence of the futile efforts at idealization made by man apart from God. Utopias have been legion. But none have offered any genuine help. All of them have sought an absolute thing instead of an absolute Person. None have been willing to admit it, that man has brought the evil upon himself. Hence only Christianity offers relief. The assurance of future justice enables the poor that are in Christ to remain "pure in heart." Comfort is theirs, genuine comfort, such as the world knows not and cannot understand. There remains a rest for the people of God.

10

THE NINTH COMMANDMENT: TRUTH

WE MAY SUM UP the meaning of this commandment by saying that it requires of us that we respect, maintain and develop the good name of ourselves and of our neighbors. The literal meaning of the words refers to swearing falsely in court. This is in accordance with the manner of promulgation of the other laws which each time mentioned the most extreme form of transgression. In this case, as in the others, we must go back from this most extreme form of transgression to the original state of affairs in order to ascertain what the positive, though unexpressed requirement was at that time.

Now in order to do this we should observe that man as God's creature and as God's image-bearer was to give interpretation to the universe. He was to seek to fathom ever more deeply the nature of created reality, of which he himself formed a part. God has expressed His ideas, His plan in this created universe. These thoughts of God, which are the truth of the created universe, was man's privilege to search out. That was to be man's science. And infinite room for expansion was there. Besides, there was real assurance of progress. The created universe was the product of God's interpretation; man could therefore be sure that his own interpretation was correct if only it corresponded to God's interpretation. If it did, man had coherence for himself as God had coherence for Himself. Thus the true scientific method was to be implication into God's interpretation. There was to be neither pure induction nor pure deduction. The universal and the particular always existed together. No detail of existence was considered apart from its center of reference in the created universe, the mind of man, and ultimately from its center of reference in the mind of God.

Man would love the truth because the truth was an expression of God's mind and ultimately was God. There was cooperation with his fellowman because each one was possessed of the same love of God.

Then at an evil hour, man would be man no more. He would fain be as God. He no longer loved God. He made himself instead of God the center of reference in what he now called his search for truth. The devil had taught men to look beyond God for truth. He held before man the delusion that one might possibly be as God. Were there not possibilities beyond God? Man was to experiment. He should no longer live by God's *ipse dixit*. History was to prove what was true.

What was the result? Failure and ruin. Man tried to be what he could not be. He was a creature and could be no more if there was to be a God. Man rebelled against this metaphysical truth. He has set himself up as a God. It was he instead of God that was to become the ultimate standard of truth. He considered his thought to be just as original and just as inclusive as God's. This was the lie. The lie is self-contradictory. Man became a house divided against itself. When he said that he might be as God, he said that possibility was higher than God. Thus God's laws, His plan, in short His affirmation was demoted. Over against it was set a negation that was just as fundamental. That seemed so innocent. Yet because God is the ultimate affirmation, no negation can be put on His level. The attempt to do so is nothing but a flat denial of God's affirmation. It was this that a creature did. The devil did it originally. He is therefore the completely self-contradictory spirit. He is self-contradictory because he contradicts God. A creature is by definition determinate. He cannot live but in the atmosphere of God's plan. For a creature to attempt to live an indeterminate existence implies his explosion. The external atmosphere is removed. He finds himself in a vacuum. Hell is the only complete vacuum. Hence in the book of Revelation, no disturbing sound penetrated from it to disturb the glory of the new heaven and the new earth. This is not due to any artificial enclosure. It is due to the paralysis of the vacuum-occupants. The devil is the metaphysical lie.

No wonder that when man identifies himself with the metaphysical lie, that he should fall into the logical lie. He has blundered and blundered sadly in his "scientific" efforts. He should have been much further along than he is. Abraham instead of Edison should have discovered the tungsten filament. Lindbergh came thousands of years too late. Man tried to study the facts apart from God. Hence he never found the true universal in human experience. He sought for no more ultimate universal than the mind of man could itself supply. And since the mind of man cannot, because he is created, function even as a secondary universal unless it be related to God the ultimate Universal, there was no unity brought into experience. Coherence became impossible for man since he sought coherence without correspondence to God. Things did not and could not correspond to the false framework of sinful thought.

Hence also, in the third place, man turned to the ethical lie, to untruthfulness, evil in the surface matter of the relation of thought and speech, to the things he knows. It could not well be otherwise. He had turned himself away from God. He no longer loved God. Hence he no longer respected himself and his fellowman for God's sake. Accordingly, when no longer true to God he no longer conceived it necessary to be true to self or fellowman. Thus society became untruthful.

Again, we should observe that the actual state of affairs admittedly does not answer fully to this picture as given. If it did, we would have hell. But that we do not is not due to man. God sent forth His common grace. It is this that gives to man some sense of metaphysical truth. He has felt some need for a beyond as a center of reference; witness the logic of idealism. This also has given man some sense of logical truth. His scientific endeavors have made some advance though blundering. This finally has given man some sense of ethical truth. The average person does not lie for the sake of lying. He has some self-respect and sense of truthfulness. In society, one may meet sometimes even a large measure of truthfulness. But all this does not in the least affect the statement that in his heart of hearts, man has allied himself with the liar from the beginning, against the truth from eternity. Jesus tells the Pharisees that they speak the things of their father whose very nature is a lie.

Accordingly, when the commandment of truthfulness comes to us in the law, it does not come to us in order to enliven the coals of common grace but to bring to fruition the gift of special grace. True, it is every man's duty to be truthful. God does not lower nor release His demand just because man has made himself impotent to fulfill it. All men should be able. Hence all men should be Christians. But the command comes primarily to those that are redeemed in order that they should bring to realization the truth that is in Him.

In Christ, man is restored to metaphysical truth first of all. Man recognizes himself as a creature of God again. Through Christ he seeks the final point of reference for his whole life in God. Man is taken out of the vacuum. The Holy Spirit has served as his respirator. Slowly man learns to breathe self-consciously.

His determinate experience revives again. Soon it operates and operates fruitfully. The new man in Christ is "set in heavenly places." That is for him the pure air that he breathes.

Thus man makes progress again. He is now in the atmosphere of logical as well as metaphysical truth. The one can scarcely be separated from the other. His progress will be slow at first. The adolescent period will be the period of his present life. Thereafter he will make his rapid strides. The new heaven and the new earth will be his and his to explore.

The chief harvest to be reaped in this life is ethical truthfulness. The Christian, i.e. the determinate human being can never, not even in the inmost depth of his thought, think of himself except in the presence of Truth. The eyes of him with whom we have to do knows no darkness. The darkest recesses of our hearts, oft hidden to ourselves, are open and naked to him. The seven spirits of God seek to make even the troubled depths of our souls fully reflective of the truth.

Hence we learn to love the truth. The truth makes us free from the thralldom of the lie.

As specific duties then, we may emphasize this internal truthfulness with ourselves. Self-examination is our daily task. And this self-examination must set the word of God as its standard. Non-Christians speak also of self-examination. Yet its results are always self-exultation or self-annihilation. The reason for this is that the world has no true standard of self-examination. It may take Jesus as an ideal man or some other ideal. The Christian has the absolute demand of the Word. He knows that the ideal is perfection, "Be ye therefore perfect even as your father which is in heaven is perfect." He knows that he is far, very far from having reached that goal. That keeps him humble. But he also knows that God's grace is in his heart and that he need therefore not despair. One day he will be perfect. Release of sin and a full knowledge of the truth lies before him. Thus he strives nobly on.

Thus we should be always more concerned with what God thinks of us than with what man thinks of us. The world tells us that we are a peculiar, that is an odd, people. We do not like to be so considered, and are tempted to become conformed to the world as far as we dare. We ask ourselves whether we can do this and can do that as Christians. Especially in this the case with all manner of worldly pleasures. Instead, God tells us that we should dare to be a "peculiar" people, in order that we may show forth the excellencies of Him who has translated us out of darkness into His marvelous light. Some of the leaders of the Jews believed in Jesus secretly, "for they loved the glory of men rather than the glory of God" (Jn. 12:42). So we dare not to align ourselves with unpopular causes, especially when the odium that would be poured upon us would come from those professing Christianity.

Then, secondly, we should not only respect ourselves as bearers of the truth, we should maintain and develop ourselves as such. Self-examination may help also for this in as such as it points us to the ideal. But above all, by yielding to the Lord who is the Spirit (2 Cor. 3:18), when He would fix our eyes on Him who is the Truth "are we transformed into the same image from glory to glory." When if, on our path of progress, there be these that seek to interfere, we may need to defend our reputation. False brethren may seek to retard our progress because our progress honors Christ. Hence for the honor of Christ we must defend ourselves. Especially is this the case if Christ has honored us by giving us an office in His church. In that case, Satan will try his best to defame us in order to defame Christ. Paul affords us a fine illustration of what to do in such a case. He received an exceptionally large amount of ridicule from the adversary because he did an exceptionally great work for Christ through the exceptional office of the Apostolate. It was his Apostleship that the enemy ridiculed. They said he was a man of wild imagination obsessed with a fixed idea. What does Paul do? He was willing to bear much otherwise, but when his office is attacked he cries out: "Am I not an Apostle, Have I not seen Christ the Lord?" "Truly the signs of an Apostle were wrought among you in all patience, by signs and wonders and mighty works" (2 Cor. 12:12).

All the while, the Christian should not present himself as being more than he is nor on the other hand needlessly lower himself before the eyes of men. And especially should he increase in the common truthfulness that even unbelievers manifest. It happens all too often that Christians are less dependable in business than non-Christians. Soon Christians have developed very flexible consciences with respect to grocery bills, weights and measures, and general business honesty. Now, this is a disgrace to Christ. It gives the world much cause to blaspheme the sacred name that is above every name.

Similar to the obligations with respect to ourselves are our obligations with respect to our neighbors. We must, in the first place, think truthfully about them. This does not mean that we must regard everyone alike. That should not be thinking truthfully. We know that some have not the truth. We know that at bottom they love unrighteousness. Yet we know that by common grace he can practice certain general truthfulness. Hence we are to "rejoice with the truth" (1 Cor 13:6). We are to "believe all things" i.e. believe all good things rather than bad things. Ungrounded suspicion is un-Christian.

In the second place, we should speak truthfully to, and about our neighbor. Thought utters itself in speech. What we say should correspond to and be expressive of what we think. Hence if we know one to be a good man we dare not say he is a bad man or not wholly a good man. On the other hand, if we know one to be a bad man we may not, for our own or his interest especially before the court, say that he is a good man. "These are the things that he shall do; Speak ye every man the truth with his neighbor; execute the judgment of truth and peace in your gates. And let none of you imagine evil in your hearts against his neighbors; and love no false oath: for all these are things that I hate, saith the Lord" (Zech. 8:16–17). Thus the talebearer who tells on no more solid basis than that of "*fema*" all manner of stories about Mr. So-and-So and especially about the Rev. So-and-So, does things hated by the Lord. For it is especially with respect to those that are in an office of state or church that we must be careful. Their reputation means much to society. In the Old Testament the judges are called "*elohim*" (Exod. 21:6); and especially Psalm 82:8, to which Jesus refers in John 10:32, "Is it not written in your law, I said, Ye are gods?" The judges were called gods because they were representatives of God, and God spoke through them. And as for those that bear office in the Church they represent God in Christ. Hence Paul's injunction to be especially careful of the reputation of those that were elders i.e. rulers in Christ's stead. Hence in all these cases, if others have spoken evil, we should, as much as within us lies, make that evil of none effect. To seek to kill false rumors may be a difficult task but a task nevertheless.

A harder task still awaits us when we observe that it is our duty to talk to others and especially to our fellow Christians about their duty to be truthful. This is most difficult when they have obviously failed in this respect. The am-I-my-brother's-keeper attitude is un-Christian. Most difficult is this task if the offender is one in high official station, but the more necessary it is that we fulfill our task. Only thus can we seek not only to respect but also to develop truthfulness about us.

For office-bearers and especially for ministers, it is necessary to remember at this juncture that in order to develop truthfulness, they must seek to elicit confessions of untruthfulness by a friendly tactful method. To be *suaviter in modo* benefits him who himself lives in a glass house. Any pretense at perfection in accomplishment will repel instead of attract. Thus one does not develop but rather retards the development of truthfulness. At the same time secrecy may be necessary. The Roman Catholic Church has with its doctrine of the *sigillum confessionis,* forbidden its priesthood to reveal the secrets revealed to them. Now, there are conceivable situations in which secrecy would be a sin. Suppose that some one should reveal a murder plot to you. In such a case the perpetrator has broken relations with society and has no right to expect anything but society's punishment.

Still further, if there is to be a general development of truthfulness in society, its members cannot in their intercourse employ any *reservatio mentalis*.

It is not always necessary to say all we know (Prov. 3:7; 29:11), but what is meant by mental reservation is the willful attempt to mislead by not speaking the whole truth. For example, someone may ask you about something you do not care to disclose. You answer him by saying that you do not know of the matter, and then mentally reserve the thought "as anything that is public." Such mental reservation is dishonesty and is productive of dishonesty.

But someone will say that we do this because it is useful for society. On this basis many moralists have defended the *mendacium officiousum*, i.e. the lie of necessity. The reasons for the defense are (a) that such lies are done for a good purpose, (b) that they avoid a greater evil, and (c) must sometimes be employed when one faces a collision of duties. Moreover, a Scripture example is cited to prove that it is permissible. The midwives of the Israelites who deceived Pharaoh were blessed. God himself told Moses to request for Israel no more than a short journey into the wilderness. Rachab the harlot who hid the spies was kept alive when others were slain. Bahurim hid David's spies in a pit and was blessed (2 Sam. 17). Now, as to the reasons given, they are not conclusive. As to the good intention, we reply that the end does not justify the means. That they avoid greater evil we cannot accept. They may avoid what seems to us a greater evil. But even Socrates knew that to lose life is not as great an evil as to court the disfavor of the gods. Nor are we ever really placed before a collision of duties. Our thinking that we are is usually due to lack of prayer and Scripture study. And if we have been faithful in these matters, there remains for the Christian little doubt but that he is walking in the Lord's ways. Then, as to the Scripture examples, we have no guarantee that the midwives were blessed because of their deception; they were blessed in spite of it for their faith. Secondly, Moses was to test out pharaoh's heart with a small request. Had he granted it, the greater matter would have been broached. Seeing he did not grant it, there was no need of broaching anything more. The case of Rachab is similar to that of the midwives. She was the only one that had faith and was saved because of it. Finally, in the case of Bahurim, we deal with martial strategy and there is no assurance that she used deception. Thus we see no reason in these examples to deviate from the strictest moral principle which has always condemned the lie of necessity.

The lie of necessity is perhaps most often practiced in the case of serious sickness. Now, we admit of course that the mental condition is important. Hence needless rudeness should be avoided. But suppose an unbeliever is sick unto death. Is it mercy to him to keep that fact from him? The knowledge of the fact might lead to repentance while the lack of knowledge of the fact might lead him to trust in his false hope again. And as for the Christian, he too has a right to die as self-consciously as possible. Difficult cases no doubt will arise, but what Christian will dare to say that God's grace will ever honor measures that are unholy?

Quite different is the case with the *mendacium iocosum*, i.e. the deception for amusement. Strictly speaking, that is no deception. The gift of imagination has enabled man to create fantastic worlds that have delighted his soul. The world of fiction is based upon it. So also in social life conversation may be enlivened by repartee that involves the *mendacium iocosum*. Yet we should observe that a free indulgence of the imaginative and romantic often makes us lose to some extent our sense of sober truthfulness and our fitness to deal with the prosaic world of reality. Even non-Christian writers have admitted that the fantastic, fatalistic, futuristic, movie presentations have helped to prepare the youth of our nation for many a career of crime and speculation. The lure of "easy" instead of "honest" money and the lure of "easy" instead of "honest" pleasure has often been evoked by disproportionate occupation with the abnormal.

Even the *mendacium humilitatis* which is usually regarded as no more than the oil that smooths the creaking joints of society may sometimes be scarcely distinguishable from hypocrisy. Too often those that are most polite will strike you "at the fifth rib" meanwhile. There is here a golden mean to strive for.

He that would be a Christian indeed should remember the words of Jesus, "I am the Truth."

11

THE TENTH COMMANDMENT: DESIRE

IT HAS BEEN POINTED out in connection with every commandment that the literal meaning of the words used in every case do not at all exhaust the import of the purpose of God. The state can expect no more than external obedience. But God is not satisfied with that. He wants internal perfection first of all.

In this tenth commandment God calls particular attention to this fact once more. The distinctiveness of this commandment is not to be found in the objects with respect to which desire is forbidden. These objects are covered by the eighth commandment. The distinctiveness of this commandment is rather to be found in its specific emphasis upon the necessity of inward perfection.

God had created man internally perfect. By whatever name we may seek to designate that which is inmost and therefore at the controls of the human life, this inmost aspect of human personality was created good. It is well to note that antitheistic thought must deny this fact. For it, there can be no ethical goodness until after the will has operated. Only the operation of the will can produce "nature" or character. Now, it may safely be affirmed that in such a case no character or nature would ever be able to develop in as much as the subject of action would be set in a vacuum, affording it no propelling power. Every subject of action must have a "nature" according to which it acts or it will starve as the proverbial donkey between two bins of hay unable to choose from which to eat. In short, a creature without a character would be no creature; he would be already metaphysically cut loose from God in whom alone he can live and move and have his being.

It is not inconsistent with this to say that the Bible itself recognizes the value and necessity of human choice in order that character should be developed. We grant this at once. The point is, however, that if anything is to be developed it must be there from the beginning. The moral cannot develop from the nonmoral. Evolution speaks much of "inherent forces" by which it seeks to maintain continuity between the moral and the non-moral, between man and the animal. On the other hand, it emphasizes the choice of the individual separated from its nature as the source of the real difference between the moral and the non-moral. This is a manifestation of the self-contradiction at the basis of non-theistic thought. Theism avoids this difficulty. It alone gives to the will of man a genuine significance because it alone gives to that will a field of operation. It would be well for orthodox Arminians to realize that they are fast playing into the hands of the antitheists by their half-way position on this point. There is no mordant power against the enemy in a position that yields half way.

We say, therefore, that the law of God was written on man's heart at creation. In his inmost desires, in the controlling forces of his personality, man was set to operate toward God. The relative priority of the intellect, the will and the feelings is not of great importance in this connection. Does the subconscious largely control the conscious? It is well. Would you emphasize with modern psychology the importance of instincts?

It is well. Would you emphasize anything else? It is well. Whatever you consider the deepest depth of human personality it is there where God wants you to be pure. And unless He had created man pure at just that point, that is, unless God has written His law on man's "heart" so that he spontaneously fulfilled that law, man could not even begin to understand what a moral commandment would be. There would be no moral reference-point in man to which commandments might be addressed. It would not be immorality but non-morality that would lead the dog to disregard your sign, "Thou shalt not steal."

Sin has set this inward core of man's personality in opposition to God. Man has sought to be the source of law instead of being satisfied to be subject *to* law. He has driven this point so far that he does not even know himself to be a transgressor of the law anymore. Without the law (that is the law promulgated at Sinai), there is no knowledge of sin. Man thinks that the sinful is the truly natural. And whatever is "natural" is said to be good. Rousseau made this the foundation of his theory of education. Hence it is necessary for us to teach that (a) the natural as come forth from the hands of God was indeed good, (b) that the present "natural" is un-natural and therefore not good.

Christ came to restore the original or true natural. He demanded perfect obedience. He emphasized this especially in the Old Testament by sending the promulgated law before Him. It was the only standard by which men could truly know themselves. Its absolute requirement was calculated to drive men to Christ as the one to fulfill its demands. Thus the law was the taskmaster to Christ. Those in Christ are perfect. They are saints. They are "free from the law." They love God anew. The core of their being is true again. "Oh how love I thy law," is the burden of their song. Hence their constant effort to trace all their motives down to their deepest lair. Thence must be driven the last vestiges of idolatry, image-worship, sabbath-breaking, disrespect to authority, human life, purity, property and honesty. No easy external satisfaction will cause them to say "all these things have I kept from my youth up." They know they have kept none of God's laws in principle. Nor do they ever divide God's law mechanically as though one commandment would be broken and the others remain untouched. Especially is this the case with respect to the first and second tables of the law. No man can love his neighbor unless he also truly loves God.

A home-sickness for heaven will be found in the Christian's heart when he looks into the tenth commandment. When will all the motives really be pure as my Lord expects them to be and as I most earnestly would have them be? Not till I am gathered with the twenty-four elders about the throne wearing the white robes of the righteousness of Christ without spot or wrinkle or any such thing. These robes no longer touch the mire of sin; they remain perfect forever in that atmosphere of righteousness.

Meanwhile, I do not forget my task as a preacher of righteousness on earth. I seek by the means of grace to develop righteousness and obedience to God's law in general, within myself and also within my fellow-Christian. And as for my fellow-man, who is not a Christian, I know that he is "dead in trespasses and sins," and hates God and his neighbor in his heart. Yet I also know that God has tempered this hatred to such a degree while on earth that it is possible for him to do "natural good." He has a certain sense of the need of law. He, to be sure, thinks that law really existed apart from God, and hence serves an unknown God, yet by this service he is kept from turning earth into hell. Accordingly, I still see in him something of the image of God, and respect the external righteousness which he does. I even cooperate with him to seek to develop a general respect for law and order, locally, nationally and internationally. By this general external righteousness, God has provided an atmosphere in which the true people of God were not at once destroyed but on which they could develop their own righteousness by grace. Thus the antithesis between the righteous and the unrighteous does not appear so clearly as we might think it would. But as time goes on, and toward the end of this world's history, God allows principle to stand against principle, the externally righteous will more and more appear to be the unrighteous. Then will that "lawless" one, "the man of unrighteousness" who exalts himself above the law of God, appear and the unrighteous will worship him and compel the righteous to worship him. But then also will He that was found worthy to open the book with the seven seals because He had been slain as the righteous one, to bring victory for righteousness to pass, appear, to cast the unrighteousness one and the unrighteous ones into the pit that is bottomless because there is no law, no order there and to receive those that obey

God's law into the realm where law and order is
and therefore rest.[15]

---

15. Van Til, C., & Sigward, E. H. (1997). *The Works of Cornelius Van Til, 1895-1987* (electronic ed.). New York: Labels Army Co.

ABOUT THE CÁNTARO INSTITUTE

Inheriting, Informing, Inspiring

The Cántaro Institute is a reformed evangelical organization committed to the advancement of the Christian worldview for the reformation and renewal of the church and culture.

We believe that as the Christian church returns to the fount of Scripture as her ultimate authority for all knowing and living, and wisely applies God's truth to every aspect of life, her missiological activity will result in not only the renewal of the human person but also the reformation of culture, an inevitable result when the true scope and nature of the gospel is made known and applied.